UNDERTOW

OF A

TRADE-WIND SURF.

GEO. H. CLARK.

HARTFORD:
CHARLES G. GEER.
1860.

PRESS OF CASE, LOCKWOOD AND COMPANY, HARTFORD, CT.

THIS VOLUME

CONTAINS A PORTION OF MY

"FUGITIVES,"

NOW RESURRECTED FROM

MAGAZINES AND NEWSPAPERS,

AND MARSHALLED IN THEIR PRESENT ARRAY

TO PLEASE MYSELF,

AS WELL AS SOME OTHERS

WHOM I WISH TO PLEASE.

A SMALL EDITION, ONLY, WILL BE PRINTED,

THE BULK OF WHICH WILL BE DISTRIBUTED

AS MY FANCY MAY DICTATE.

AS A FEW COPIES WILL PROBABLY BE FOR SALE,

I Dedicate

THE BOOK TO THAT SMALL PORTION OF

The Public

WHO MAY READ OR

BUY IT.

CONTENTS.

7

OLD SONGS.

WHO shall deny the poet's heart
   The memories of joys and tears,
That mingle as he reads apart
   The treasures of his earlier years?

There is in half forgotten rhyme
   A charm that makes the singer thrill,
And lingers, in life's twilight time,
   Like sunset o'er a distant hill.

As travelers, when the day is spent,
   Look back upon the pleasant scene,
Review each path by which they went,
   Each shady nook and bit of green,

So does the musing rhymer love
   To ponder over labors past,
And on each recollected verse,
   A glance of fond affection cast.

2

Or as a kindly father loves,
  Beneath the tender evening skies,
To fondle all the little doves
  That make his home a Paradise,

So will the poet cherish lays
  That underneath his hand have grown,
Partly for that his neighbors praise,
  And partly that they are his own.

He loves them when he sends them forth
  On seas of printers' ink to sail,
And loves them when the daily press
  Receives them with a welcome hail.

And when some critic's eye is caught
  By sly or humorous words of mine,
And noting the sarcastic thought
  That underlies the quiet line,

All pleasantly reprints the same,
  With pungent paragraph of praise,
I call him friend—and drink his health,
  And wish him joy and length of days.

And as the flying years go by
  And cast upon my rhymes a shade,
When friends have nearly all forgot
  The ripple their appearance made,

'Tis very pleasant once again
   To see the village papers seize
And start afresh the stranded waifs,
   To fly before a favoring breeze.

Slight as they are, I love to meet
   The old familiar look they wear,
And though eclipsed by brighter stars,
   Still love to see them glimmer there.

And I am conscious when I read
   My words to metered music set,
That I can write a daintier song
   Than any I have written yet.

Then let the poet's fancy play
   In secret o'er his hoarded rhyme,
Nor take from him the slender ray
   That gilds the cold gray wing of Time.

WELCOME TO WINTER.

BRIMMERS to Winter! Winter wild and weird,
  Frost-crowned and peerless! To his jocund laugh
And frolic eye, and long white flowing beard,
  Let us with right good will our bumpers quaff.
For why should poets paint the jovial sage
  So fiercely grim, and not his beauties sing?
Why call him blear eyed, crabbed, curst with age,
  And slander thus the good old roistering king?

Not so do we behold him. Glowing hearts
  Welcome with joy their ancient loving friend,
While he ungrudgingly to them imparts
  Pleasures that multiply withouten end.
Who brings delights to wile the evenings long?
  Who drives off cares that pained the summer time?
Who crowns long months of toil with mirth and song,
  But brave old Winter in his lusty prime?

Hark to the sleigh bells on the snow-piled plain—
　Their witching music fills the frosty air;
While riant voices, like a gay refrain,
　Tell that red lips and sparkling eyes are there.
And mark yon skater on the ice-bound stream—
　Such magic circles spring beneath his heel,
And such his dexterous feats, we almost deem
　Some tricksy Ariel rides the ringing steel.

I love hoar Winter for the boisterous glee
　With which he ministers to young and old;
A bounteous gentleman indeed is he,
　Who comes with joys and blessings manifold.
He lends new beauties to the maidens fair,
　That they the more may captivate our hearts,
And he it is, not Cupid, that should bear
　The twanging bow and the resistless darts.

Where should Love's home be but around the hearth
　Where great fires up the ample chimney roar?
When care is banished, and light-hearted mirth
　Brings forth for us his long-time hoarded store.
Grandsire and sire, all garrulous with delight,
　Their rugged features brightening in the blaze,
Grow young again, and fill the ear of night
　With tales and legends of the olden days.

Though winds may rave, and the wide drifting snow
  Give to the shrouded world an aspect drear,
'Tis home's triumphal hour; and the rich glow
  Of rosy love beams all around us here.
Hail to brave Winter! Honored be his name!
  The bard, delighted, lingers on the theme,
Forgetful of Ambition, Fortune, Fame,
  While Love, heart-throned, sits here and reigns supreme.

AUTUMN LEAVES.

In the broad forest leaves are falling—
    Their gathered dead
The hinder'd brook fantastic walling,
While the pert squirrel, sharply calling,
    Rains down the mast from overhead.

Old oaks, their lordly branches lifting,
    Stand bald and bare;
And crimson leaves, in shadows shifting,
With slumberous sound go slowly drifting,
    Drifting along the cumbered air.

Sunlight, down through the foliage leaping,
    Rich 'broidery weaves;
In the wide openings onward sweeping,
It falls in holiest beauty, sleeping
    On greensward slopes and eddying leaves.

Then look, my saddened soul! around you,
    And ponder o'er,
If, when Life's autumn leaves have found you,
And the grave-mounds of friends surround you,
    You too shall droop to rise no more.

Like to those leaves about me flying,
    In mid air tossed,
The body then, no more relying
On its strong bulwarks, will be dying,
    Its fire in smouldering ashes lost.

But death cannot destroy the spirit,
    Which is eterne!
Then, trembling soul! no longer fear it;
You, who no dying doom inherit,
    Should for a new existence yearn.

Fit hour for deep and mournful musing,
    Is Autumn time;
With pregnant thoughts my soul infusing,
It asks, while leaves their hold are losing,
    Were not those dead ones in their prime?

NOVEMBER.

Again, O month of melancholy,
  Full of pale thought and sad presage,
Thou callest up each youthful folly
  To haunt me in my pilgrimage.
Why urge with hollow voice and cold,
  Disheartened manhood to remember?
I *feel* that I am growing old
  Without thy warning, drear November.

Wild and remorseless winds are singing,
  In mournful tones, the dirge of Summer,
While the hoar-frost is broadcast flinging
  The blight of an unwelcome comer.
I meet you now, alas! to sigh
  O'er times I cannot but remember,
When ye, O cheerless winds, and I
  Met in a happier past November.

3

Thou dost evoke in swift transition,
 A shadowy and tumultuous throng
Of scenes, that once were all Elysian,
 And pure as Eden's morning song;
But only with malicious smile
 To ask if I youth's hopes remember,
That have been tombed this weary while,
 Back in a long, long gone November.

Thou bring'st me not my promised pleasures.—
 The dead leaves fall with plaintive sound,
And, like those leaves, life's hoarded treasures
 Fall withering on the waste around.
Tears, tears obstruct my sight, and thou
 Dost plague my soul with thy "Remember,"
As all forlorn thou meet'st me now,
 A pilgrim gray, O bleak November!

LIFE'S MERIDIAN.

As when, at noon, some traveler tired,
  Rests on the summit of a hill,
But with the glorious prospect fired
  Keeps heart and spirit buoyant still,

Till toward the land he has to tread
  He bends his weary steps once more,
Where forests dark and wide o'erspread
  The hills and plains that stretch before;

So, like that traveler, now I stand
  A moment at life's noon-day place,
Where rises Memory's spectre band,
  And Hope averts her pallid face.

Yet do I take my pilgrim staff,
  Resolved youth's promise to fulfill,
Although life's best and brightest half
  Is past—for I have climbed the hill!

Passion is dead, and Hope betrayed;
  Thought deepens o'er my clouded brow;
I've lost the substance for the shade,
  And Love is but a memory now.

With higher thought and purpose yet,
  I will pursue my journey on;
I cannot, if I would, forget
  The lesson of my half life gone.

Up, up faint heart! Be very bold,
  Nor linger in the race of life;
Still on! nor let your faith grow cold,
  Nor waver in the coming strife.

Undaunted still, beside the brave
  Press onward, with the goal in sight,
Nor falter till ye reach the grave,
  And bow to its o'ermastering might.

WINTER RHYMES.

Come, wheel the arm-chair to the fire
   That blazes bright and high,
While the storm raves and howls without
   And fills the gloomy sky:
Let shrieking winds outside the door
   Play out their gusty part,
So long as comfort reigns within,
   No winter chills the heart.

Then let the storm, love, ring alarms,
   We've happy hours in store;
If God but lends us hope and health,
   Why need we ask for more?
Riches bring heavy thoughts and cares—
   No jot for gold care I,
I have a sunshine of the heart
   That wealth could never buy.

Give me these welling founts of love—
   These authors quaint and old,
And in such goodly companie
   How valueless is gold!
How sweet the dew from noble thoughts,
   Poured out in honied rhyme,
Falls on the thirsty mind, and wakes
   The soul to themes sublime.

Heeds he the pudder overhead,
   Or noise of driving sleet,
Who calleth up such pleasant friends
   Around his hearth to meet?
Ah no! with chosen books like these
   My heart is full of glee,
And Night, that sends such storms abroad,
   Brings happiness to me!

NO MORE.

WHAT time the woods were glorious in decay,
   And gentle airs the fallen leaves were heaping,
In radiant Autumn, at the close of day,
   While dreamy Silence on the air sat sleeping,
Poor truant Thought a holiday was keeping;
   Hope smiled, and Memory ran its tablets o'er,
And Love a harvest of sweet thoughts was reaping,
   When to my ear there came the words "No MORE!"

"No MORE!" Whence comes that vague mysterious cry
   To break the charm of my delicious musing?
To bring dismay with its unapt reply,
   The impatient heart's enthusiast hopes refusing?
Some mischief-loving elf, its power abusing,
   Has sent perhaps its gloomy voice before,
And with strange prescience my mind perusing,
   Thus vexes me with its forlorn "No MORE!"

Like frost to flowers it fell upon my thought,
 And chilled my throbbing life-blood to its center;
Within my heart a sudden change it wrought,
 And seemed my soul's most hidden depths to enter.
"Is this," I asked, "some lonely wood frequenter,
 Some Dryad who his fate does here deplore,
Or is it some weird fiend or dark tormentor,
 That with sepulchral tone thus cries 'No MORE?'"

"Tell me," I said, "thou mocker, will youth's high
 Wild aspirations come no more to meet me?
Nor with impulsive flight stoop from the sky
 With lofty schemes to cheer but not to cheat me?
Will not bright Hope hold out her hands to greet me,
 And wreath my brow with garlands, as of yore?"
The prophet voice, returning to defeat me,
 But rendered back the baleful sound "No MORE!"

"And what art thou, that thus with hollow voice
 Obstructs the light that o'er my heart was gleaming?
Hope lingers yet, my loved, my earliest choice,
 And sits enthroned in peerless beauty beaming;
Say, is she not still full of youthful seeming,
 And will she not yet triumph as before—
Her promises to youth in age redeeming?"
 Shuddering I hear the dread reply "No MORE!"

But friends are left me still—and they will come,
  Boy-hearted, while I am life's vale descending;
Surely, among them all, there will be some—
  My old familiar friends—who will be bending
Kind eyes on one who feels the fate impending.—
  Will youth and love be ours beyond the shore,
Dark, silent, drear, to which my barque is trending?—
  The ghost returns his dolorous "No MORE!"

Deep in my heart-cells sinks the awful word—
  A shadow falls upon my spirit's yearning;
Thoughts, dread and solemn, in my breast are stirred
  Of perished joys that know of no returning.
The fearful warning in my brain is burning,
  And all seems stranded on a barren shore,
While the blind Future, all the Present spurning,
  Rings a remorseless knell in its "No MORE!"

GREENWOOD.

AND this is Greenwood! These
Its woods, and hills, and vine-embowered dells,
    Where venerable trees
Lift their swart limbs above Death's sculptured cells.

    Green is the turf below,
And green the coronal of boughs o'erhead,
    Where shimmering sunbeams glow
And gild the silent city of the dead.

    Flecked with the sunset's rays,
Yon stately pillar tells its solemn tale;
    And through the distant haze
Memorial shafts rise dimly from the vale.

    Though sweet buds blossom here,
And birds in ecstacy of music soar,
    Yet it is ever drear
To muse where Death has garnered up his store.

Here crush beneath the tread
Flowers that derive their fragrance from the mould
 Where rest the crumbling dead,
And where corruption's worms their banquet hold.

 On every side one sees
Great marble jaws, all yearning for their prey,
 And marks the festering lees
Of mouldering corses oozing from the clay.

 Pale, ghastly forms arise,
All featureless and grim, in sickening crowds,
 Whose fixed and hollow eyes
Glare from dark skulls in mockery of their shrouds.

 Methinks the air, as well,
That drifts among these monumental stones,
 Comes tainted with the smell
Of charnel-houses and of dead men's bones.

 Let me not linger here—
For thoughts too gloomy round my fancy play,
 And cast a shadowy fear
Upon the soul, that should be bright alway.

THE OLD YEAR.

ONWARD, still onward blindly urging,
  With booming voice sublime,
One fragment more falls, downward surging
  Into the Gulf of Time;
Falls, with a sound of woe and groaning,
  From its returnless host,
As with a sad and grievous moaning
  The year gives up the ghost.

All frosted o'er with rime, and hoary,
  Time droops his palsied head;
From his thronged realms is heard the story,
  The story of the dead.
See how his path is tracked with sadness,
  With scenes of poignant grief—
Some fainting in their hour of gladness,
  Some in the ripened sheaf.

Over her first-born yearned a mother—
　How boundless was her joy!
Swift fell the gloom her joys to smother,
　Death came and claimed the boy.
One hour her breast was as a fountain
　That bore Love's rosy glow,
The next, it heaved beneath a mountain
　Of overwhelming woe.

A dreamer, almost faint with blisses,
　Gazed on his plighted love;
Such raptures blended in their kisses
　As have their source above:
A night of darkness and of sorrow
　Rolled on its sombre tide,
And when he woke to hail the morrow,
　The angels had his bride.

I saw an ancient man and holy,
　A Soldier of the Cross,*
Who at his Saviour's feet knelt lowly,
　And deemed earth's honors dross;
Whose cheek, although his head was hoary,
　Still wore its youthful bloom,
Go, full of years and christian glory,
　Down to the waiting tomb.

*Dr. Milnor.

We cannot but lament with weeping
  Mortality's last claim,
While memory has the deeds in keeping
  That sanctify his name.
O such as he make up the leaven
  That gives the world its worth,
And great the gain to him and Heaven
  That is such loss to earth!

Brim full of gloomy thoughts and saddening,
  The old year breathes its last;
The only feeling left that's gladdening
  Is, that its cares are past.
High hopes, wild thoughts, and earnest dreaming
  Along its track are spread,
And even Fancy's fondest scheming
  Lies mingled with the dead.

And I, whose heart with hopes was throbbing
  One little year ago,
Now in lone desolation sobbing,
  Mourn for their overthrow.
The burning thought, whose vivid flashes
  Were kindled in my breast,
Expiring now sinks into ashes
  And leaves me all unblest.

GROWING OLD.

In the lapse of years our hopes grow dim,
  Our warm affections cold—
Yet how unwilling to confess
  That we are growing old.
Life's morning sun in beauty burst
  Upon our opening view,
And thought was pure and holy then,
  Bright-winged and ardent too.

The buoyant pulse beat strong and free
  In that dream-woven day;
Brave were the hearts, and bold the deeds
  That pressed their eager way;
And though we saw that others failed,
  Our faith grew not the less—
What man had done we dared to do,
  Nor dreamed but of success.

Where are those aspirations now?
  Our visions, where are they?
They people Memory's wilderness,
  Lorn victims of decay!
The electric thrill we rendered back
  To beauty in our youth,
Is ours no more. Love folds his wings
  And saddens into truth.

And now, indeed, how bitter 'tis
  To look into the past,
And see the shipwrecks of our joys
  Bound in its barriers fast:
And O how drear to feel that Time
  His iron heel has pressed
On our enthusiast hopes, and crushed
  The strongest and the best.

This is the thought that fires the brain
  With keen and poisonous art—
That wrings the life, with tightening grasp,
  From out the weary heart:
Yet here we cling with desperate force,
  Amid the sickening strife,
For time, who steals our years away,
  Takes not the love of life.

THE AUCTIONEER.

'TIS even so. Experience proves the truth of the idea,
That Life is but a great vendue, and Time an auctioneer;
Where man is tempted by his hopes some rueful lots to buy,
As all who've reached their spectacles can safely testify.

He's fond—this ancient auctioneer—of mystifying folks,
And fobs them off with bitter fruits, wrapped up in funny jokes:
For sometimes when you think you've bought a pleasure mighty cheap,
The very memory of the trade's enough to make you weep.

I have been favored in my time, like many witless wights,
With glimpses at the Elephant, and other wondrous sights:
But never dreamed the cost would be so fearful in amount,
Until this wheedling auctioneer brought in his long account.

For instance;—for some youthful pranks I'm charged a shining crown;
(But not the golden kind that weighs the wigs of monarchs down—)
A crow's-foot under either eye, and furrows on my brow,
And corns upon my pedal farm that grow without the plough.

5

And manhood made some purchases that did'nt turn out well—
The memory comes to plague me now with its lugubrious bell;
For human passions had their play, and poached in strange preserves,
And left me with a visual haze and vibratory nerves.

It's always so—the goods are bought, no matter what the price,
The buyer all the blessed while being sure they're cheap and nice;
But when the bill is handed in—the "little bill" it's called—
The stoutest heart that ever beat might well shrink back appalled.

Yet still the ambidextrous rogue keeps hammering at his trade;
He has so many customers he's never long delayed:
He scores a great lumbago, now, against a pleasant sin,
And leaves his victim with a smile that curdles to a grin.

A postliminiar draft he holds, this meddling diplomat,
Which must be met when it matures—there's no evading that.
As well might you the ancient dame's aerial project try,
And sweep with a terrestrial broom the cobwebs of the sky.

Yon fool with such a sallow phiz secured a lot abroad—
Went to enjoy it, and came back bejeweled like a lord;
But now, poor man, he's looking round to buy another lot;
A smaller one will serve his turn—it's easy to be got!

And he who has the shaky limbs, and totters in his gait,
He says he is'nt ready yet—the auctioneer must wait.
He thinks it very hard to be so badgered with a bill,
And swears he does'nt owe the scamp a solitary mill.

At all such warning finger-posts we look with heedless eyes,
And sugared pleasures tempt us yet, as sweets inveigle flies:
For Time's a cunning auctioneer who knows his business well,
And always has the thing we want, and always wants to sell.

And so for some poor foolish toy we barter all our powers,
And for a minute's worth of fun lose many precious hours:
Yet if we bid the fearful price that gains us wealth or fame,
We only leave the bankrupt's pawn—a protest and a name!

THE ANNOYER.

AGAIN that unmelodious drum
  Disturbs the quiet street,
Tag, rag and bobtail following on
  With shouts and clattering feet.
For why? The little man behind,
  In military boots,
Appareled like a warrior bold,
  Is beating up recruits!

Red havoc's voice is in my ear,
  Its trappings meet my eye,
And th' flesh is creeping on my bones
  To hear the summons nigh.
O would yon gleaming sword were hung
  Where it might gently rust,
And that poor flag be laid away
  To gather mould and dust.

Oh why entrap the harmless man
  Who owns those precious pegs?
A soldier's march would surely cramp
  His parenthetic legs.
Can there be valor in the soul
  That lights such eyes as those?
No, no—but like a silly sheep
  He to the shambles goes.

Pray tell the dear deluded man
  Whom music has beguiled,
What sacrificial human bones
  On battle fields are piled:
Or hint that desperate feats of arms
  On Montezumaen farms,
May prove a total loss to him
  Of both his feet and arms.

That weary drum! O wrap it up
  In its protecting flag;
And in the fifer's squeaking tool
  Be pleased to stuff a rag:
Or if you must keep up your din,
  Pray choose another beat,
And give your patriot feelings vent
  In some remoter street.

If you'll be kind enough, my lad,
　To do that friendly thing,
I'll write a rousing song for you
　In furlough times to sing;
I'll even do a better deed,
　My noisy friend, than that,
And for your special benefit
　Will pass around the hat!

MONTEREY.

"And every body praised the chief
  Who such a fight did win."
"But what good came of it at last?"
  Quoth little Peterkin.
"Why that I cannot tell," said he,
"But t'was a famous victory!"

NEWS of a battle fought and won—
  Victorious, we have swept the field!
Our camp-fires light the flying foe,
  And we his captured weapons wield;
While swooping through the sulphury air
  The vultures come to claim their prey,
And banquet on the dead who fought
  The murderous fight of Monterey.

Unfurl the banners, torn and wet,
  That led the serried columns on;
The sight perhaps will lend a glow
  To pallid cheeks and features wan.
Wave them as tokens that the slain
  In one wide grave are laid away,
Safe from the prowling wolves that snuff
  The tainted air of Monterey.

Heed not the widow's blistering tears,
  Nor heed the orphan's sorrowing cries,
But let your clamorous voices drown
  The mournful undertone of sighs.
Why should pale weepers stand apart
  And shed such earnest tears to-day?
Do they not hear the gladdening shout
  That hails the news from Monterey?

It makes our languid pulses leap,
  It stirs and thrills our kindling hearts,
'Till we, responsive, join the cry
  That such unwonted joy imparts.
Then let the bells loud 'larums ring,
  And lavish flags their folds display,
For a glorious victory is achieved
  Under the walls of Monterey.

The bugle's peal, the rolling drum,
　　The scattering shots, the wild hurrah,
The trampling hoofs, the frenzied rush,
　　The noise of conflict heard afar;
The tattered banners, scorched but UP!
　　The shouts, the shrieks of wild dismay,
The thundering cannon's distant roar
　　Proclaim the fall of Monterey!

Through streams that pour a crimson flood,
　　'Mid sabre-strokes and volleying flame,
Wading in life-warm pools of blood,
　　The victor tracks his way to fame!
The hour of triumph comes at last—
　　The smoke of battle rolls away,
And he, all gore incarnadined,
　　Looks grimly down on Monterey!

Come, ye forlorn and smitten ones,
　　Whose hopes of yesterday are cold,
Come join the cheerful groups who weave
　　Bright garlands for the heroes bold;
For breaking hearts and human love
　　And tears must be subdued to-day,
And hushed the sigh that heaves the breast
　　For kindred slain at Monterey.

6

In vain perhaps such deeds may fill
  Th' alembic of the poet's rhyme,
Yet some memorial will they claim
  To shield them from sarcastic Time.
Then rear—'twill be a proper pile
  To chronicle the glorious day—
A cenotaph of human skulls
  And bleaching bones from Monterey.

And leave the tower pyramidal
  In naked truthfulness to stand,
An emblem and a record too—
  Fit archive for a Christian land.
It will a stern memento prove,
  Without the scholar's quaint display,
Nor needs a blazoned tablature
  To tell the tale of Monterey!

MY BOY.

"There is even a happiness
That makes the heart afraid."

ONE more new claimant for
    Human fraternity,
Swelling the flood that sweeps
    On to eternity.
I, who have filled the cup,
    Tremble to think of it,
For be it what it may
    I must yet drink of it.

Room for him into the
    Ranks of humanity;
Give him a place in your
    Kingdom of vanity.
Welcome the stranger with
    Kindly affection,
Hopefully, trustfully,
    Not with dejection.

See, in his waywardness,
  How his fist doubles,
Thus pugilistical
  Daring life's troubles;
Strange that the Neophyte
  Enters existence
In such an attitude,
  Feigning resistance.

Could he but have a glimpse
  Into futurity,
Well might he fight against
  Farther maturity;
Yet does it seem to me
  As if his purity
Were against sinfulness
  Ample security.

Incomprehensible,
  Budding immortal,
Thrust all amazedly
  Under life's portal;
Born to a destiny
  Clouded in mystery,
Wisdom itself cannot
  Guess at his history.

Something too much of this
 Timon-like croaking;—
See his face wrinkle now,
 Laughter provoking:
Now he cries lustily—
 Bravo! my hearty one!
Lungs like an orator
 Cheering his party on.

Look how his merry eyes
 Turn to me pleadingly;
Can we help loving him,
 Loving exceedingly!
Partly with hopefulness,
 Partly with fears,
Mine, as I look at him,
 Moisten with tears.

WELAWAY.

O softly blows the southern breeze
　　Beneath the window-blind,
And plumes its winnowing wings for one
　　It never more may find.
The birdling that you seek, O wind,
　　In your Æolian play,
Some wandering seraph, stooping, saw,
　　And bore to Heaven away.

You took your flight, O southern breeze,
　　When Summer's sheaves were bent,
And there was sorrowing round my hearth
　　When your sweet joyance went;
Ah! little did I know how much
　　Of happiness was left,
Until of that new love of ours
　　My sad home was bereft.

He went when Autumn's golden light
  The glowing world o'erspread,
And left behind a night of gloom
  And rayless dark instead.
Life was not life to me, unless
  His presence formed a part,
For he was the irradiate light
  And day-spring of my heart.

At sound of my familiar step
  How brightened all his looks;
Down went the playthings, and away
  Went all his pictured books;
His little hands like fluttering wings
  Were tremulous with joy,
And, happy in each other's arms,
  The father clasped his boy.

We lived and loved—a blessed life!
  As we shall live no more,
For angel pinions bore him off
  From this despairing shore:
The cloud that shut him from my sight
  Cast back a fearful spell,
And made my quailing spirit shrink
  Where its dark shadow fell.

Blow softly, gently, southern breeze,
  Amid the buds and bloom,
And let your odor-laden airs
  Search all the quiet room;
You cannot find his sweeter breath,
  Nor his red lips restore,
And though you gladden other hearts
  You wring my own the more.

I read aright the moaning sigh
  Beneath my window-blind—
It is the loving sprite who seeks
  For one it cannot find;
For one whose bright and starry eyes
  Are distant now and dim,
While Memory fills its vacant halls
  And corridors with him.

O God! that such a world as this,
  So beautiful and brave,
Should be of all our fondest loves
  And dearest hopes the grave:
That in one bitter hour, a blight
  Should change its glorious hue,
And wither beauties, which no showers
  Nor spring-time can renew!

MY TWILIGHT HOUR.

I was quietly sitting last night by myself,
Musing partly of poetry, partly of pelf;
Of what would be said of my yesterday's rhymes,
And how I should weather these very hard times;

When by easy transition Thought wandered up stream,
To the time when young Life was a beautiful dream,
And amid the remembrances, some how or other,
Came the spectacled eyes of my stately Grandmother.

Ah, well I remember those silver-rimmed specs,
And the sharp eyes behind them, my plans to perplex;
And the quaintly crimped cap, bordered neatly with lace,
That so daintily edged her benevolent face.

Fine gold were the beads that her neck gaily bore—
Though long out of fashion yet treasured the more;
For they were dumb speakers, and whispered of him
Whose fond recollections her eye could bedim.

7

Her hair had been black, but Time has a way
Of touching such locks with his pencilings gray;
Although neither he, nor his yoke-fellow, Care,
Could conquer her will, nor its action impair.

Well skilled in the art our wild natures to school,
Now mild in her sway and now stern in her rule;
O well did we boys in those juvenile days
Know her promptness to punish, her proneness to praise.

But the Spoiler o'ertook her at length in the race,
And the power of his grasp left a visible trace;
Her strength, from long buffeting, finally failed,
And her spirit before the new enemy quailed.

Ah! well—she has gone where her troubles are o'er,
Where sorrow's dark wing casts a shadow no more;
And there she has met with *my* fountain of joy,
My own lovely angel, my darling, my boy!

And are they together—my young love and old?
Do her arms my lost treasure in rapture enfold?
O, eyes of my dear one! look down from the sky,
And tell me those arms are around you on high.

Ye stars—homes of all that we mourn here as lost—
Send a ray to my heart that with anguish is tossed;
And tell me that I shall yet meet, where you roll,
The dove-eyed young cherub now torn from my soul!

FAR AND NEAR.

Sitting by my open window,
  Looking out where day is waking,
I remember him who left me,
  As a gloomier dawn was breaking.

Here before me, green and fragrant,
  New-mown lawns stretch into distance,
While the elm trees, wooed by breezes,
  Palpitate with love's resistance.

Trembling to the zephyr kisses,
  All the dewy foliage glistens,
And the oriole sings his matin,
  Where the charmed thrush sits and listen

Birds of gay and glittering plumage
  On triumphant wings are soaring,
Songs of joy and exultation
  Over all the young dawn pouring.

Soft, transparent clouds are floating,
　White as wool, or amber tinted,
Where celestial robes of wonder
　By their lustering folds are hinted.

Far beyond the skyward warblers
　I can hear angelic voices;
Through the blue my vision reaches,
　And my lifted soul rejoices.

All sublimed, up springs my spirit,
　Mounting on seraphic pinions,
Gazes on the loved and lost one,
　Meets him in supreme dominions.

There, in Love's eternal mansion—
　There, where Death is lost in distance,
I can see my own sweet darling,
　I can join his new existence.

Thus my strayed but cherished first-born,
　Gone, I could but wonder whither,
Draws me with electric forces,
　From earth's grossness upward thither.

His the hands that mine are clasping—
　His the voice that hails my greeting;
His and mine the olden rapture,
　The remembered joy of meeting.

EXTRACT.

Sweet Fancy loves to play with trifling themes,
And loves to revel in the land of dreams,
On every zephyr's breath her pinion stirs,
And earth, and air, and all the clouds are hers.
Her pictures rival, in their mystic wreaths,
Those which the sprite on winter windows breathes;
She floats with moonbeams over fields of snow,
Which starbeams interlace with diamond glow:
When spangles glisten in the frosty air,
She's up and off to frolic with them there;
She loves the dreamy haze of autumn hills,
And loves the music of the singing rills.
She floats with sunbeams through the shimmering trees,
And bends to hear the murmuring hum of bees:
She loves all quiet beauties and sweet sounds,
As on light wing she goes her airy rounds.

The phosphorescent glow, like flashing steel,
That following foams around the parting keel;
Celestial rainbows, circling after storms,
The crimson flush their wrestling clouds that warms;
The songs of birds that hail the blushing morn,
The plashing rain of summer evening born,
The booming melody of far off bells,
Whose undulations throb along the dells;
The insect hum that stirs the drowsy noon,
The new-mown hay of aromatic June;
The apple blossoms, and the bursting rose,
The odor-laden breeze that comes and goes—
O'er these her influence frail Fancy flings,
And waves in dallying wantonness her wings.
Hers is a realm of unalloyed delight,
Radiant with beauty, and with star-gems bright;
The sparkling dome enroofs her ample hall,
And where Thought radiates, there she halos all.

IMAGINATION takes a broader sweep—
A wider circle and a bolder leap;
She loves the seething ocean's crag-piled shore,
With its wild grandeur and perpetual roar;
She loves its breakers, and delights to ride
Its crested surges and its rampant tide,
While its great tones, upheaving and elate,
Seem kindred voices calling to its mate.

The hollow moan of hidden mountain floods,
The fierce winds battling with the crashing woods;
The storm-king bursting from his awful throne,
With eyes of lightning, and with thunder tone;—
Where'er roused Nature shows her mighty power,
There will Imagination proudly tower.
She springs exultant in her upward flight,
And plumes her way o'er many a giddy height;
When her imperial pinions mount the gale,
Thought, quivering, leaps, to follow on the trail.
Through fields of light, beyond the arching blue,
Her winnowing wings allure the heavenly dew.
When startled Reason flings to her the helm,
Worlds are her kingdom, space her subject realm;
Down the long vista of the coming years,
On victor wing her steady way she steers,
Reads there events as prophets read of yore,
And rides triumphant through the misty frore.
No hurtling clouds nor blinding storms of hail
Can make her strained and flashing eyeballs quail—
Above, beyond the lazy course of time,
She holds her way, majestic and sublime!

And MEMORY has her triumphs, and her trials,
As she turns back the hands upon the dials;
Strikes chords that give a long forgotten tone,
And claims the past, dominion of her own.

All there is hers—the over-peopled past,
Where sleep dead hopes, our earliest and our last;
She calls at will our youthful longings up,
Fills to the brim Remorse's wormwood cup,
Strikes the wild string that Passion could not break,
'Till its remembered tones once more awake;
Touches the spring that opens young desires,
And once again they thrill along the wires;
Lifts the dark curtain that enfolds young Love,
And purpling sunbeams gild it from above.

Full to o'erflowing is her dark domain,
Where awful Silence and pale Sorrow reign.
Tomb of lost joys and sepulchre of hopes,
Wherein the aching soul bewildered gropes;
Faith, Hope, and Love against the portal lean,
While one lone Phantom stalks across the scene.
Down the dim aisles, and o'er the crumbling walls,
No starry beam, nor ray of sunlight falls;
Impending clouds shut down from overhead,
And wrap in gloom that region of the dead!

THE OAK.

Yes, blot the last sad vestige out—
  Burn all the useless wood;
Root up the stump, that none may know
  Where the dead monarch stood.
Let traffic's inauspicious din
  There run its daily round,
And break the solemn memories
  Of that once holy ground.

The hallowed spot your fathers long
  Have kept with jealous care,
That worshippers from many lands
  Might pay their homage there:
You spurn the loved memento now,
  Forget the tyrant's yoke,
And lend oblivion aid to gorge
  Our cherished Charter Oak.

8

'Tis well, when all our household gods
   For paltry gain are sold,
That ev'n their altars should be razed
   And sacrificed to gold.
Then tear the strong tenacious roots
   With vandal hands away,
And pour within that ancient crypt
   The garish light of day.

Let crowds unconscious tread the soil
   By Wadsworth sanctified;
Let Mammon bring, to crown the hill,
   His retinue of pride;
Destroy the patriot pilgrim's shrine—
   His idols overthrow,
Till o'er the ruin grimly stalks
   The ghost of long ago.

So may the muse of coming time
   Indignant speak of them,
Who Freedom's brightest jewel rent
   From her proud diadem;
And lash with her contemptuous scorn
   The men who gave the stroke,
That desecrates the place where stood
   Our brave old Charter Oak!

THE BLACKSMITH

'TIS evening. At his sombre trade
  The burly blacksmith sings,
While underneath his rapid strokes
  The sounding anvil rings:
The hot and glowing iron bar,
  As his strong hammer swings,
A sudden shower of fiery sparks
  Athwart the darkness flings.

Now giveth he the hardening steel
  A keenly tempered edge ;
Now by his lusty blows is wrought
  The rough and clumsy wedge;
Anon aloft, with mighty strength
  He whirls the ponderous sledge,
Which falls, as falls a catapult,
  The massive bar to swedge.

The water in the cooling trough
  Looks black along the brim,
Where, peeling from the plunging bar,
  The hissing cinders swim.
The roaring fire emits a glow
  That lights his visage grim,
And brings to view the wondering boys
  Who come to gaze at him.

Quite powerless in his sturdy grasp
  Stands yonder stubborn ox;
He claps him in a wooden vise,
  And turns its leathern locks;
And having thus suspended him
  In quadrupedal stocks,
Nails up his hoofs with less remorse
  Than joiners nail a box.

Our blacksmith is a jovial man,
  Who loves a quiet joke,
And sometimes at the village inn
  His thirsty clay will soak;
And once, upon town-meeting day,
  He took the stand and spoke,
And raised three cheers for Harry Clay,
  And sundry groans for Polk.

Such was our blacksmith:—but alas!
　He glads our eyes no more:
He left for Californian mines
　In search of golden ore;
He left his bellows by the forge,
　His tools upon the floor,
And left beside, I blush to say,
　A wife and children four.

THE PARSON.

WHEN I was young and fond of noise,
  And wore my first gray homespun jacket,
And fought stout battles with the boys,
  And filled my father's house with racket,
Our well-beloved pastor died,
  And left behind him scores of weepers—
Stout pillars of the church, long tried,
  As well as lesser props—and sleepers.

He was a patriarch, wise and gray,
  One of the old time christian scholars;
Who cheered affliction's weary way,
  And gave th' oppressed advice—and dollars.
The matrons' love for him, at last,
  Sublimed almost to veneration,
For he'd baptized one-half the past
  And all the present generation.

Outside the church, the good man held
  A comprehensive supervision,
And village quidnuncs were compelled
  To bow before his calm decision.
Though party strife might rage and swell,
  Or skeptics raise some knotty question,
There came no storm he could not quell,
  No doubt too grave for his digestion.

I do remember well the scene,
  When, all the congregation seated,
He closed the book with reverend mien,
  And twice the pregnant text repeated;
And then, as influenced from above,
  His heart with holy themes expanding,
Appealed to Faith and Christian Love,
  As well as human understanding.

His looks, his tones, his earnest ways
  Form one of memory's pleasing pictures,
As he, in strong but homely phrase,
  Imparted hope or uttered strictures.
The velvet cap he always wore,
  Whene'er he thumped the pulpit cushion,
Loomed like a beacon from the shore,
  To warn us sinners from perdition.

The best of men a cross must bear—
  So providence or fate contrive it;
Of private griefs he had his share,
  And some that were not quite so private.
He might conceal the smouldering fire
  Of mental or domestic trial,
But troubles with the wrangling choir
  Were patent as their own bass-viol.

Of course, there was among his charge
  One busy, meddling, ancient maiden,
Who like a fire-ship roamed at large,
  With furtive store of scandal laden.
She scattered brands of discord free,
  She slandered and annoyed the parson,
Till all agreed she ought to be
  Indicted for constructive arson.

On Wednesday night he always made
  To us a quiet pastoral visit;
So when the bell his touch betrayed
  My Mother never asked "who is it?"
But wheeling out the easy chair,
  With its inviting arms of leather,
She laid his pipe, with thoughtful care,
  And steel tobacco box together.

Those genial times were mellow ripe,
   When folk were not inclined to bicker,
If ministers enjoyed a pipe
   And sipped a social glass of liquor;
So while his cheerful features glowed,
   And smoke-wreaths circled to the ceiling,
His talk in streams of wisdom flowed,
   Like waters from a fount of healing.

We loved the man, revered him too—
   As who did not that ever knew him?
His piety and kindness drew,
   With cords of love, all classes to him.
His praise by men need not be lipped
   To make our sorrowing hearts beat faster,
For memory holds a secret crypt
   Wherein is shrined our sainted Pastor.

9

A PICTURE.

'TIS but a picture—just a bit
  Of canvas touched with paint—
Where I can see, amid the trees,
  A gable old and quaint;
A skiff that swings beneath the bank,
  A distant mountain peak,
A summer sky where all is blue
  Except one crimson streak.

It is the place where in my youth
  I used to laugh and play—
O long ago, before I dreamed
  Of love-locks turning gray.
There is the broken wall through which
  Stray cattle used to pass,
And the same sheep I used to chase
  Are nibbling at the grass.

There stands the meditative cow
  Knee-deep in August mud,
Whisking the same old burry tail,
  And dining on her cud:
And underneath the willow tree
  That droops above the stream,
A horse, with sympathetic droop,
  Leans lazily to dream.

At rest along the village green,
  The morn's ablutions done,
The silent geese, with sentry set,
  Are winking at the sun;
And just before the school-house step
  The hens are in the dirt,
Upheaving pungent clouds of dust
  With unexpected flirt.

And in the $\vee$ which forms the fence
  That symmetry defies,
A frisky colt is kicking at
  The pertinacious flies;
While just upon the other side,
  In funniest sort of heap,
Three petted calves, with frequent stretch,
  Are growing in their sleep.

The air is in a slumberous calm;
  No leaf nor twig astir;
The very partridge roosts as if
  She never meant to whirr.
No cat nor dog is now abroad,
  No bird is on the wing,
And even Katydid forgets
  Domestic woes to sing.

The foot-path through the pasture lot
  That skirts the alder clump,
And leads across the bubbling spring
  By yonder ancient stump,
Has lost its morning power to tempt
  My languid steps that way,
As underneath the spreading elm
  In clover heaps I lay.

I know the spot—it takes me back
  To days of Indian bread,
When I had very slender feet,
  And quite a largeish head;
The head had little in it then,
  And never ached, as now—
But Time has figured out a sum,
  Like Daboll's, on my brow.

There was no shadow on my path
  In that remembered day,
Nor did I know how sad it was
  To have a note to pay;
Then grandma always favored me
  With purest milk for lunch—
But I've got bravely over that,
  And take it now in punch!

PLACE BY THE SEA.

I HAVE found just the spot that I wanted,
  The place I have looked for so long,
Where the climate is really enchanting,
  The air full of unwritten song.
Where the women are riant and rosy,
  And dress as their grandmothers did,
Where the old folks are happy and cosy,
  And children behave as they're bid.

It's a place by the edge of the ocean,
  With the charmingest sort of a beach,
And picturesque rocks on the margin,
  Which the billows are chafing to reach;
Where the meadows slope down to the breakers,
  And breakers dance up to the land—
The debateable region between 'em
  A surf-beaten crescent of sand.

Serene are the skies of the summers,
  As Italy ever could boast,
And sweet is the breath of the breezes
  That hallow the loveable coast.
The surf, booming over the ledges,
  The dreamiest melody makes,
That comes to the ear like the murmur
  The sea-shell forever awakes.

The place is remarkably quiet,
  Where steam whistles never are heard;
Where the plover is tame as the robin,
  The woodcock a let-a-lone bird.
It's too far away for the sportsman
  To come with his pestilent gun,
And too great a distance from railroads
  For lovers of fashion and fun.

The men are not talking of dollars,
  Unless they have something to sell;
And go to a church every Sunday
  That boasts neither organ nor bell.
The women are simple and modest,
  Though willing enough to be seen,
But would shy at the last style of bonnet,
  And blush at a stiff crinoline.

There the sea air gives relish to chowder;
   There apples will keep into spring;
There the rot is unknown to potatoes,
   And corn is a very sure thing.
The chickens you find on the table
   Are old-fashioned pullets, and fat,
And the lamb that you get is not mutton—
   And surely there's something in that.

No telegraph startles the dreamer
   With news of the shocking and vile,
Though a newspaper, printed in Boston,
   Enlightens folk—once in a while!
No Irishman comes with his blarney—
   It's out of the way of his priest—
And of all the inducements to tarry
   This last is not one of the least.

Moreover, they tell me that never
   Was poverty known in the town;
That the poorest have money invested,
   And pay for their purchases *down*.
It follows that one thing is lacking,
   And that's a poor rhymer like me:—
So I think I will pack up to-morrow
   And go to that place by the sea!

EVENING BY THE SEA.

THE gold and crimson flush of day
    Has faded from the west,
And evening's breezes rise and play
    Along the ocean's breast;
The waves come rolling to the shore
    With low and mournful sound,
As if strange footsteps on its floor
    Were echoing around.

Thin mists are gathering on the deep
    In vapory folds of light,
And, as along its verge they creep,
    Seem spirits of the night,
Arising from their hidden caves,
    Far down the depths of green,
And resting on the surging waves
    Their silver crests to screen.

10

The giant rocks, in gloomy pride,
　　Frown down upon the main,
And their swart shadows in the tide
　　Frown darkly back again.
The long and level sandy beach
　　Fades narrowing out of sight,
As if its yellow sands might reach
　　Beyond the wall of night.

The far-off sky that spans the world
　　Bends in a broader arch,
While clouds beneath it are unfurled,
　　Gray in their upward march:
They lose themselves the stars among,
　　That seem but looking through,
As if the smoke of incense hung
　　Along the dome of blue.

The vesper star is burning bright
　　In dazzling beauty now,
As if it softly stooped to light
　　Old Ocean's wrinkled brow;
A beacon set within the sky
　　By an Almighty hand,
For angel hosts to journey by
　　Through yonder blessed land.

At such a still and lonely hour,
  Beside the restless sea,
The presence of an unseen power
  Seems hovering over me;
Strange undulating waves of sound
  Pass trembling overhead,
And leave a silence so profound
  My soul is filled with dread.

FROST WORK.

WHAT proof is there that Autumn, with its sheaves,
  Is such a sad and melancholy season?
Though bilious poets mope among its leaves,
  That's no good reason!

Say you the gusty winds forlornly sigh,
  And fill the air with lamentable wailing?
Well, so do lovers when their hearts beat high—
  Yet they're not ailing.

The gipsy squirrels make the pleasant wood
  To echo with their freaks and merry gambols;
For they delight, as all good fellows should,
  In Autumn rambles.

The burly bees, those wanderers far and free,
  Are waxing lazy now that summer's over;
For even bees don't always want to be
  Living in clover.

See from yon creaking press the fragrant must
  Foams in the vats, in circles wide and wider,
Making mouths water, and frail mortals lust
  After new cider!

Then strew the way with idyls and bucolics—
  Hail to nut gatherings and Thanksgiving musters!
Welcome ye "apple-bees" and husking frolics,
  Where beauty clusters.

 *   *   *   *   *

Adorned with gorgeous leaves—O say not sere!
  The forest leans against the mountain hoary;
Of all the glorious scenes that crown the year
  The crowning glory!

Give me my strolls in Autumn's brown arcades,
  My moonlight loiterings in dismantled arbors,
And sighs may burthen antiquated maids
  And pensive barbers;

Or ease the Miss who pens a new "romaunt,"
  And melts in tears o'er her poetic riches,
But whose cerulean hose betray a want
  Of friendly stitches!

OLD ROBIN.

WHAT time the wheat was in the ear,
  And all the flax was bolled,
Within the breasts of ROBIN's friends
  Funereal bells were tolled.

Faint, silver bells—unseen, unheard,
  Except by those alone,
Whose hearts the pensive cadence drank
  And echoed back its tone.

And who is ROBIN, that young hearts
  Are thus disturbed for him?
For whom unwonted lips are pale,
  And eyes with moisture dim?

Alas! he was their favorite Horse—
  The loved, the true, the tried;
The horse that never ran away,
  And never, never shyed!

Then pause and listen, Fanny dear,
  While I the tale rehearse,
And here embalm his memory
  In horsepitable verse.

He was indeed a noble steed—
  Of honored stock was he,
Who up, far up the stream of time
  Could trace his pedigree.

On regimental training days
  He was a goodly sight,
As with a trampling hoof he rushed
  Into the thickest fight.

The stirring music of the drum,
  The shout of soldiers grim,
The clash of arms, the cannon's roar,
  Were a delight to him.

But this was ROBIN'S patriot side,
  His holiday address;—
Behold him at his daily tasks
  And love him not the less.

With conscious look and lively pace,
  As if his work were play,
Sagacious ROBIN, true as steel,
  Pursued his even way.

If reason blends with instinct's powers
  Let learned doctors tell;
But it is true that ROBIN knew
  Each gentle playmate well.

And when around his littered stall
  The noisy children ran,
His voice proclaimed his happiness
  As plain as whinny can.

And every day their love for him
  Still strong and stronger grew,
While he returned each fond caress
  With horse-affection true.

But these delights are over now,
  And love alone abides;
For all his warrior work is done,
  And all his peaceful rides.

Ah! never more his answering neigh
  The listening ear shall fill—
He sleeps in peace beside the brook
  That washes Copper Hill.

And I, who've known him long and well,
  His gentleness and worth,
Who oft have heard his praises sung
  Beside his master's hearth,

I act the Minnesinger's part—
  The mourning harper play,
And from my sympathetic heart
  Pour this elegiac lay.

11

ALBUM VERSES.

You ask me for an Album rhyme
    In such a modest sort of way,
I'm doubtful if my pen this time
    Should have its usual lawless sway.

Well—we will see. No dainty dreams
    Adorn my dull poetic shelf,
And so, for lack of livelier themes,
    I'll write about the book itself.

A lady's Album, now-a-days,
    Is like the quaint Kaleidoscope,
Where brilliants out of pebbles blaze,
    And clearest amber springs from soap.

Where locks of hair, too red to burn,
    Outvie the plumage of the dove,
And lumps of lead, all blushing, turn
    To statues of the God of Love.

Dry wisps of oaten straw will change
   To Cupid's emblematic darts,
And kidney beans, with impulse strange,
   Swell straightway into throbbing hearts.

Here sentimental wheys and curds,
   Whipped in the poet's frothy strain,
Rise all sublimed—like simple words
   Delivered in brave Pistol's vein.

And cooing turtles on their nest
   Outrival peacocks in their cries,
While sighs that heave the lover's breast
   Like Ætna's lava belchings rise.

Turn the machine—the leaf I mean—
   And what is only common ore,
Will shine like nuggets that are seen
   By wanderers on Pactolus' shore.

If boys and girls who write, alas!
   For this Kaleidoscopish book,
Would squint but once behind the glass,
   They'd never take a second look.

Love's flame would smoulder into smoke,
   Wild Passion's flood exhale in gas;
Eternal vows turn out a joke,
   And every lover prove an ass.

TO A CAGED LION.

MONARCH of India's burning plain!
Where once in undisputed reign
   Thou held'st despotic sway;
Lord of the desert once, and King—
Thou who a dauntless glance could fling
   Back to the god of day!
There's terror still upon thy brow,
And pomp about thee, even now.

How great, how fallen! Caged and chained
By him on whom thou once disdained
   To cast contemptuous look;—
Those iron bars, that narrow floor,
The confines of that prison door,
   How can thy spirit brook!
Throbs yet thy all unconquered heart
As when it played the monarch's part?

Methinks, when fettered in a cage,
With one resistless roar of rage,
　　And madness uncontrolled,
Thy great heart, at the very first,
Should in its agony have burst
　　Beneath the captive hold.
Worthy thy life, old King, would be
Such death to set thy spirit free.

Yet here thou art, shut up and cramped,
With all thy haughty ardor damped,
　　Ignobly shown about;
A terror to each childish fear,
The subject of full many a jeer,
　　From many a rabble rout—
A living lesson to the world,
How low a monarch may be hurled.

Yet all thy greatness is not fled—
Thou hast a solemn, measured tread,
　　As in thy loftier days;
Majestic still thine eye-balls flash,
That sternly mortal eyes can dash
　　When they return thy gaze.
Thou art Imperial!　And no chains
Can base the blood in royal veins.

Say what they may, thy spirit dwells
Unconquered still—and freedom swells
   Within thy breast till death:
Thou, as thy sires, wast born to rule,
And thy King-passion cannot cool,
   But with thy latest breath:
Though servile chains around thee cling,
Still art thou "every inch a King!"

THE MENAGERIE.

Did you ever! No, I never!
  Mercy on us, what a smell!
Don't be frightened, Johnny dear—
  Gracious! how the jackalls yell!
Mother, tell me, what's the man
  Doing with that pole of his?
Bless your precious heart, my dear,
  He's stirring up the beastesses.

Children, don't you go so near:—
  Heavengs! there's the Afric cowses:
What's the matter with the child?
  My! the monkey's tore his trowses.
Here's the monstrous elephant—
  I'm all a tremble at the sight;
See his mighty toothpick, boys—
  Wonder if he's fastened tight?

There's the lion—see his tail!
　How he drags it on the floor;
Sakes alive! I'm awful scared
　To hear the horrid creature roar.
Here's the monkeys in their cage,
　Wide awake you are to see 'em;
Funny, aint it;—how would you
　Like to have a tail and be 'em?

Johnny darling, that's the bear
　As tore the naughty boys to pieces;
Hornéd cattle!—only hear
　How the dreadful camel wheezes!
That's the tall giraffe, my boy,
　Who stoops to hear the morning lark—
'Twas him who waded Noah's flood,
　And scorned the refuge of the ark.

There's the bell! The birds and beasts
　Now are going to be fed;
So my little darlings, come,
　It's time for you to be abed.
Mother, 'tis'nt nine o'clock—
　You said we need'nt go before;
Let us stay a little while—
　Want to see the monkeys more!

Cries the show-man, "Turn 'em out!
  Dim the lights! There, that will do;
Come again to-morrow, boys,
  Bring your little sisters too."
Exit mother, half distraught,
  Exit father, muttering "bore!"
Exit children, blubbering still,
  "Want to see the monkeys more!"

12

THE WEDDING.

ALL solemnly the wily priest
   Stood by with his abettors,
Conspiring how to bind two hearts
   In everlasting fetters.

And while to reach the chancel rail
   The groom his bride was leading,
No mortal raised a warning voice
   To stay the rash proceeding.

The smooth divine then subtly wove
   His magic web around them,
And firmly knit the tightening coils
   That mystically bound them.

He caught them by their christian names,
   Artistically clever,
And with an ambidextrous twist
   Entangled them forever.

The relatives looked calmly on,
  Nor any harm mistrusted,
But with a strange composure saw
  The fatal noose adjusted.

The last support being knocked away,
  The lady and her lover
Plunged headlong into married life,
  And all the show was over.

A slight sensation stirred the crowd,
  Who murmured an "amen," sir,
As though the law and gospel too
  Were satisfied again, sir.

The victims then were borne away
  Beyond the reach of warden,
With feelings near akin to those
  Who traveled over Jordan.

The rail-car seized them in its jaws,
  While we looked on in horror, ·
Persuaded that no man could tell
  Where they would land to-morrow.

Well, let them go. It's all too late
  For respite or repentance,
As Heaven's celestial telegraph
  Has registered the sentence.

THE RAIL.

I MET him in the cars
  Where resignedly he sat;
His hair was full of dust,
  And so was his cravat;
He was furthermore embellished
  By a ticket in his hat.

The conductor touched his arm
  And woke him from a nap,
When he gave the feeding flies
  An admonitory slap,
And his ticket to the man
  In the yellow-lettered cap.

So, launching into talk,
　　We rattled on our way,
With allusions to the crops
　　That along the meadows lay—
Whereupon his eyes were lit
　　With a speculative ray.

The heads of many men
　　Were bobbing as in sleep,
And many babies lifted
　　Their voices up to weep;
While the coal dust darkly fell
　　On bonnets in a heap.

All the while the swaying cars
　　Kept rumbling o'er the rail,
And the frequent whistle sent
　　Shrieks of anguish to the gale,
And the cinders pattered down
　　On the grimy floor like hail.

When suddenly a jar,
　　And a thrice repeated bump,
Made the people in alarm
　　From their easy cushions jump
For they deemed the sound to be
　　The inevitable trump.

A splintering crash below,
  A doom-foreboding twitch,
As the tender gave a lurch
  Beyond the flying switch,
And a mangled mass of men
  Lay writhing in the ditch.

With a palpitating heart
  My friend essayed to rise;
There were bruises on his limbs
  And stars before his eyes,
And his face was of the hue
  Of the dolphin when it dies.

        *   *   *

I was very well content
  In escaping with my life,
But my mutilated friend
  Commenced a legal strife—
Being thereunto incited
  By his lawyer and his wife.

And he writes me the result,
  In his quiet way, as follows;—
That his case came up before
  A bench of legal scholars,
Who awarded him his claim
  Of Fifteen Hundred Dollars.

MEDITATIONS

THOU man of Fez, of Bagdad and Morocco—
   Thou lotus-eater on the dreamy Nile:
Who, undismayed, hast met the fierce sirocco,
   And courted danger with a quiet smile,

This, then, is YOU! Begirt with scarf and turban,
   Your hand light resting on a sabre's hilt,
An oriental nomad! Yet half urban,
   Enough to show no Yankee blood is spilt,

Nor yet dried up, nor changèd its natural courses:—
   But still pulsating through your vigorous veins,
The native heart obeys its native forces,
   True to its own remembered hills and plains.

And you have wandered through old Egypt's valleys,
   And floated, spell-bound, on the moon-lit Nile?
Fanned by the breeze that with the daylight rallies,
   To fill the sail that shades your brow the while:

Where Pyramids repose in classic grandeur,
　Where Memnon stands, but speaks no more at morn;
Land where the curtain fell on Park and Lander,
　Just as its folds were opening up the dawn.

Land of strange mysteries and stranger knowledge,
　More beautiful that distance makes it dim,
Shadowed by that old time, when ne'er a college
　Granted diplomas to an Isis grim.

Who now shall follow up those unknown waters,
　And pluck the secret from that country's heart?
And tell if Africa has lovely daughters,
　Dwelling amid yon mountain air apart?

They wait the advent of some gallant Bayard,
　On whose warm lip to press the electric kiss,
Fraught with the influence of an orient Naiad,
　To link fair Cleopatra's time with this.

What undiscovered realm you next will write of,
　No breathing mortal guesses now, nor knows;
But we may hear from you as soon in sight of
　The Ural mountains or Kamtschatka's snows.

Perhaps from Eden's bowers of primal roses—
　Or—still more distant—from a frail balloon,
Whose wings shall bear you where you may touch noses
　With him who sways the Empire of the Moon!

Well, go your ways. But ere you go forever,
　To wander thro' strange lands that now lie darkling,
Give us one Lecture more, bold, bright and clever,
　Instinct with life, and, like old Nilus, sparkling.

Then will we say, "God speed you!" And at parting
　Bestow our benediction, brief but solemn—
The hope still growing, from your hour of starting,
　That we shall meet again—in your next volume!

13

THE PORTRAIT.

'Tis very odd—and yet there is
  A slight resemblance too:
Although a stranger well might ask
  If this were meant for you.
There's too much roundness to the cheek—
  The lips are all too red;
And those are natural curls, my love,
  That glorify the head.

The maid has such a conscious look
  Of bashfulness and fun,
That one would guess her half coquette,
  And half demurest nun:
Or deem some merry devil lurked
  Within those angel eyes,
To tempt deluded man astray
  With hopes of paradise.

And did you really, truly wear
  That charming bodice-waist,
With its provoking open front
  So exquisitely laced?
If low-necked dresses then were made
  So wonderfully low,
Pray tell me why it is that now
  You never wear them so?

How could an artist ever gaze
  Upon those glowing charms,
Nor throw his frenzied brush away
  To clasp them in his arms?
Yet he might paint you as you sit
  Beside the cradle now,
Without a tremor of the hand,
  Or flush upon his brow.

Well, never mind. Although the hair
  That droops beneath your cap
Has lent its gold to that young rogue
  Who slumbers in your lap,
Yet when the baby's grown a boy,
  And wears a jaunty hat,
You then may say to him, that once
  His mother looked like that!

I REMEMBER.

I REMEMBER, I remember
 The school-house on the hill,
And the floggings that I there received
 Live in my memory still;
And IT remembers me as well,
 For where the scholars sat,
My name upon the bench is carved
 In letters long and fat.

I remember, I remember
 How at the play-spell hour
The Deacon's apples disappeared,
 That were so green and sour,
And how the haymow kept them safe
 'Till they were mellow grown,
And fragrant as a dewy rose
 That is but newly blown.

I remember, I remember
  My precious mother's care,
How she would scour my Sunday face,
  And comb my tangled hair;
And O the pennyroyal tea—
  Dread colic's antidote!
And all the bitter stuff she poured
  Down my rebellious throat.

I remember, I remember
  The cake I used to crib,
And the dark room where they shut me up
  Whene'er I told a fib!
And do I not remember well
  The supple twig of birch,
That tingled on my back, when I
  Did not behave at church!

I remember, I remember
  The long bright holiday,
And all the little ragged boys
  With whom I used to play;
We, in those frolic hours of glee,
  Were boys together then,
But now I find, to my surprise,
  Those little boys are men!

"THE GOOD OLD TIMES."

THE glorious Autumn comes again,
  With voices full of glee,
But I am sad—for times are not
  As once they used to be;
When all the girls wore homespun gowns,
  And shoes with leather strings,
And never thought of crinolines,
  And such expansive things.

Once I enjoyed the Autumn days
  Among the upland trees,
Where chestnuts by the bushel fell,
  With every passing breeze,
And reached my home at supper time
  With bag or basket full,
To find the mug of cider there
  For me to "take a pull!"

And there were dreamy evening hours,
  In cold and frosty weather,
When we before the cheery fire
  Were seated all together;
The women with their knitting work,
  The boys with each a book,
"Old Bose" asleep upon the hearth,
  And puss within the nook.

But now I spend the weary nights
  Unfriended and alone,
And hear no more the hearty laugh
  At jokes in banter thrown:
I gaze into my stupid grate
  And picture old times there,
And only wake to find the scene
  A castle in the air.

O how I long for such good times
  As once I used to know,
When not a girl at singing-school
  But liked me for a beau:
For every thing I knew is changed,
  From its accustomed look,
Except my old Arithmetic
  And Webster's Spelling Book!

TO A CITY PUMP.

O PUMP! that workest with an iron will,
  (Thy well forged handle justifies the phrase—)
I've known thee long, and come to try my skill,
  Though late, in weaving stanzas to thy praise.
The neighboring housemaids know thee too, full well,
  And oft have fondled thy familiar spout,
While jaunty aprons swiftly rose and fell,
  In unison with arms, red, bare and stout.

And now, O pump! thou'rt robed as winter is,
  Ice-ribbed and crowned with tiara of snows;
The frost, grotesque, illumes thy sober phiz,
  And tips with pendant icicle thy nose.
The overflowing and abundant tide,
  Frozen in dangerous hillocks at thy feet,
Gives careless comers an unlucky slide,
  When bruiséd heads untender curb-stones meet.

The vigorous plying of incessant hands
  Hath worn thy handle till it shines amain,
And thy poor nozzle, clasped by brazen bands,
  Will soon be sought by wondering maids in vain.
Thy blessings have been bounteously poured out,
  Morn, noon and night, through many a weary day,
'Till time and use have quite destroyed thy spout,
  And left thee now an emblem of decay.

Ye Naiad votaries of this frail machine,
  Pause, and reflect upon its fallen state!
Time's warning finger on the Pump is seen,
  Which points no less to your impending fate.
Bethink you, slipshod nymphs! and thinking, pray
  That when life's sorrowing troubles all are o'er,
You may awake to hail a brighter day,
  Where toil shall cease, and pumps be worked no more.

Decay strides onward with resistless power:
  Man trembles at the dread destroyer's name,
And at the last inevitable hour
  Sinks in dismay, and owns its awful claim.
Kings, empires, worlds, obey the great behest,
  And disappear beneath the stream of time,
Submerged, in one incongruous mass to rest,
  With thee, O Pump! and this elegiac rhyme.

14

TWILIGHT.

An hour for meditation,
  For calm and quiet thought,
When, sometimes, bright ideas,
  But oftener colds are caught.
No nightingales are waking
  To charm us with their jugs,
But the air is full of beetles
  And other lesser bugs.

There are predatory night-hawks
  Like omens in the air,
And multitudinous fire-flies
  Are blinking every where.
The torch-like summer lightning,
  Guides Thetis to her bed,
While her disappointed lover
  Is grumbling overhead.

The breath of the syringoes,
   Incomparably sweet,
Is mingled with the odors
   From gutters in the street;
The westering breeze is laden
   With uncongenial savors—
Too liberally dispensing
   Its complicated favors.

The moonlight in the tree tops
   A silver tissue weaves,
While the caterpillar army
   Is fattening on the leaves;
And a nervous pair of cat-birds,
   Who inhabit yonder nest,
With a matrimonial squabble
   Are preparing for their rest.

Thus sitting by my window,
   Where the gaunt musketo sings,
I am suddenly made aware of
   A rushing pair of wings;
And an ugly apparition
   Upsets the table mat,
And on the floor lies sprawling
   'A palpitating bat.

Now comes in requisition
  The duster and the broom,
And the blundering vile intruder
  Is ejected from the room.
But the tender hour of twilight
  Is tender now no more,
As the streams of perspiration
  Adown my forehead pour.

The affinity to gas-light
  By insect fiends displayed,
Bids me close my open window,
  As a sort of barricade.
Good night to zephyr breezes,
  To moonbeams and to bugs—
Good night to fragrant roses,
  And their enemies the slugs.

COCKNEY LYRIC.

AGAIN is Spring's delicious breath
　　All over this gay world of ours,
Awaking from their winter's death
　　Green grass, and buds and fragrant flowers.
You busy cloud its drapery spreads,
　　And with the dallying south wind flirts,
'Till the big drops beat on our heads—
　　Wrung fitful from its trailing skirts.

Ah, how refreshing is the rain,—
　　Heaven's sponge is squeezed, and lo! the flood,
While cooling heated streets again,
　　Turns whirling wreaths of dust to mud:
It drips upon my Sunday hat,
　　It wrinkles my cravat askew;
It crimps my well starched collar flat,
　　And soaks my trowsers through and through.

But now the pleasant shower is past—
 The kindly sun looks out once more,
And blades of grass start up, aghast,
 By gutter's edge and cellar door;
Scant samples of dame nature's dress—
 They meet my meditative gaze,
'Till dreams of Jersey come to bless
 And set my fancy in a blaze.

So journeying by the zigzag stairs,
 (Almost as crazy as my rhyme,)
Above the city's poisonous airs,
 Up to the house's top I climb.
And what a glorious sight to see—
 This mighty mass of brick and mortar,
From Bull's Head to the Battery,
 Encircled all around with water.

So Moses stood on Pisgah's height,
 And viewed afar the long sought scene,
In rapture there beheld the sight,
 With Jordan's swelling flood between,
This be my Pisgah! And at hand,
 (My Jordan,) rolls fair Hudson's wave,
Where dear Hoboken—promised land!
 Stoops down its jewelled front to lave.

A CHARGE OF INFANTRY.

Betsy's got another baby!
  Darling, precious little tyke!
Grandma says—and she knows, surely—
  That you never saw its like.
Isn't it a beaming beauty—
  Lying there so sweet and snug?—
Mrs. Jones, pray stop your scandal;
  Darling's nose is *not* a pug!

Some one says 'tis Pa all over,
  Whereat Pa turns rather red,
And to scan his features, quickly
  To a looking-glass has fled;
But recovers his composure
  When he hears the nurse's story,
Who admits, that of all babies
  This indeed's the crowning glory.

Aunt Belinda says she guesses—
   Says indeed she knows it *poz*—
That 'twill prove to be a greater
   Man than e'er its father was;
Proving thus the modern thesis
   Held by reverend doctors sage,
That in babies, as in wisdom,
   This is a progressive age.

Uncle Tom looks on and wonders
   At so great a prodigy;
Close and closer still he presses,
   Thinking something brave to see.
Up they hold the babe before him,
   While they gather in a ring,
But alas! the staggered uncle
   Vainly tries its praise to sing.

As he stares, the lovely infant,
   Nestling by its mother's side,
Opes its little mouth, and smiling,
   Gurgles forth a milky tide.
Uncle tries to hide his blushes,
   Looks about to find his hat,
Stumbles blindly o'er a cradle,
   And upsets the startled cat.

Round about the noisy women
   Pass the helpless stranger now,
Raptured with each nascent feature,
   Eyes and mouth and chin and brow;
And for this young bud of promise,
   All neglect the rose in bloom,
Eldest born, who, quite forgotten,
   Pouts within her lonely room.

15

THE SEWING MACHINE.

"GOT one? Don't say so! Which did you get?
One of the kind to open and shet?
Own it yourself? How much did you pay?
Does it go with a crank, or a treddle—say?
I'm a single man and slightly green,
Tell me about your sewing machine."

Listen, my boy, and hear all about it.—
I don't know how I could do without it.
I've owned one now for more than a year,
And like it so well I call it "my dear!"
'Tis the cleverest thing that ever was seen,
This wonderful family sewing machine!

It's none of your notable Wheeler things,
With steel-shod beak and cast iron wings;
Its work would bother an hundred of his,
And is worth a thousand!—Indeed it is.
And has a way—you needn't stare—
Of combing and braiding its own back hair!

Mine is not one of those stupid affairs
That stands in a corner with what-nots and chairs;
And makes that dismal headache-y noise,
Which all the comfort of sewing destroys;
No rigid contrivance of iron and steel,
But one with a natural spring in the heel!

Mine is one of the kind to love,
And wears a shawl, and a soft kid glove;
Has the merriest eyes, and a dainty foot,
And sports the charmingest gaiter boot,
And a bonnet with feathers, and ribbons, and loops,
And any indefinite number of hoops.

None of your patent machines for me,
Unless Dame Nature's the patentee;
I like the sort that can laugh and talk,
And take my arm for an evening walk;
That will do whatever the owner may choose,
With the slightest perceptible turn of the screws!

One that can dance, and—possibly—flirt;
And make a pudding as well as a shirt:
One that can sing without dropping a stitch,
And play the housewife, lady or witch:
Ready to give the sagest advice,
Or do up your collars and things so nice.

What do you think of my machine?
Better than anything else you've seen?
It isn't a stiff mechanical toy,
But supple, and lithe, and warm, my boy!
With a turn for gossip, and household cares—
(Which include, you know, the sowing of tares.)

Tut, tut—don't talk. I see it all;—
You needn't keep staring so hard at the wall;
I know what your fidgety fumblings mean—
You would like, yourself, a sewing machine!
Well, get one then;—of the same design—
There were plenty left where I got mine.

THE GEOLOGIST TO HIS LOVE.

SOME busy gnome has been at work
   With cabalistic art,
And changed to yielding pumice-stone
   My fossiliferous heart,
Which seems to be as tender now
   As crumbling mica-slate,
While its component parts are in
   A strange transition state.

Your charms are pictured on my brain
   In carboniferous words,
As plainly as on Hadley rocks
   The tracks of ancient birds.
And strata of new feelings, love,
   Crop out as strong and bold
As sandstone from the hillside crops
   Above the rocks of old.

And through my daily life there runs
  The most delightful thoughts,
As runs a thread of precious ore
  Through cold auriferous quartz;
And as the secondary rocks
  The primal overlap,
So this alluvial sentiment
  Is quite distinct from trap!

Beneath your gaze, I do believe,
  Basaltic boulders thrill,
And that Mount Tom itself would throb
  Obedient to your will.
So might your glances turn a brick
  To purple amethyst,
And change to passion's willing slave
  A cold geologist.

The humid rays your eyes emit
  Would warm a stalagmite,
And their ethereal hue outvies
  Prismatic iolite.
Then look with favor, as I thus
  Impulsive break my mind,
As I would break a block of flint
  Medæval life to find.

I have no doubt that love can claim
  Volcanic origin,
And that th' arterial fount is where
  Its subtle fires begin.
Its calide permeates all my life,
  As lustre does the spar,
And courses through my tingling veins
  Like fumes of cinnebar.

Then prithee fix the happy time—
  The incandescent hour,
When coral artists shall arise
  To deck our bridal bower;
And if some tender aerolites
  Should answer Hymen's knock,
We'll classify the specimens,
  My love, as cradle rock.

PISCATORY.

My thoughts had been so long of earth,
   I sought for scenes to vary 'em,
So, pondering, stopped awhile to look
   At Mr. G.'s aquarium.
The clear transparent wall of glass
   Displayed an odd interior,
As full of life, if not as wide
   Or deep as Lake Superior.

Uneasy bullheads, up and down,
   Gyrated through the lucid flood,
In search of their lost Paradise,
   An Eden of congenial mud;
Like poor forlorn Evangeline
   They waste their days in vain endeavor,
And emulate that dreary maid,
   In wandering to and fro forever.

The military perch is there,
  With his portcullis on his back,
And where his bristling armor comes
  The lesser rabble clear the track;
Then troutlings have a sudden call
  To start for some remoter sphere,
And the young minnows seek the shade
  Of green umbrageous foliage near.

The lazy lizard moves, and shows
  His fingered hands and human eyes,
That might beguile a nurse to wait
  And listen for his baby cries.
But lift your microscopic tube,
  And what an awful change is there—
A monstrous dragon looms in sight,
  Enough to stir St. George's hair!

Around the pebbles at their base
  The shrubs their feeble rootlets coil,
Beneath the infant shad, that swims
  Unconscious of a future broil.
While flattened out against the glass
  An idle slug tenacious clings,
Like to a blind repulsive bat,
  Without his ribbed and leathery wings.

Within this narrow lake I see
  The life that ocean dwellers live,
Where infusoria is the meat,
  The only meat their markets give.
But ah, I miss my bivalve friends,
  And search in vain the shallow sea,
To find the high-born oyster maid
  That loved a clam of low degree.

And thereby hangs a sad, sad tale
  Of aqueous loves, and hopes, and fears,
That well might heave your tender breast,
  And fill your gentle eyes with tears.
Some other time I may rehearse
  The tragic tale—and tell you how
The wretched parent slew the clam—
  But have no heart to do it now.

BOB.

Dear Robert, we have been good friends
   From youth to lusty prime,
And you have lent me sage advice
   In prose, full many a time—
Which small account I now propose
   To liquidate in rhyme.

The women deem a single man
   A misanthropic thing,
Who ought to 'tend a turnpike gate,
   Without a chance to swing,
And never hear a marriage bell
   'Till he a belle shall ring.

The world is full of waiting girls,
  And you are in the wrong,
When you prevent from willing lips
  The sweet hymeneal song,
And hear instead the plaintive cry,
  "Why tarries he so long!"

'Tis something more than monotone—
  This passion-breathing sob,
And seems designed of pleasant dreams
  A bachelor to rob;
So prithee take one to your arms
  And make her happy, Bob!

It even stirs our married nerves
  To see the pouting girls
Spreading their nets and crinolines,
  And letting down their curls,
And radiating smiles enough
  To melt the iciest churls:

To see the jaunty gaiter boots
  Along the pathway trip,
And, where they clasp the silken hose,
  A tantalising slip
Of 'broidery, that provokes the sight
  At every dainty dip.

Much more should it distract the man
　　Who only dreams of bliss,
Nor knows the thrill that permeates
　　A matrimonial kiss,
Which he may freely give and take,
　　Yet never give a-miss.

We know that your accomplishments
　　Are not so very rare,
And that you cannot even play
　　Nor sing "Begone dull care:"—
Yet with a wife you'd duet soon,
　　And improvise an air!

Moreover, you must need a wife
　　To see to shirts and things,
And keep you from the pokerish path
　　That's full of traps and springs,
As well as to protect your cash
　　From its proverbial wings.

A man may have a noble head,
　　A tongue that hates a fib;
A form to please Praxiteles,
　　And money bags *ad lib.*,
But what's the use of all these gifts
　　If he's without a rib?

Don't flout me with the fox, who wished
  His friends to share his pain;—
That this is not a case in point
  Is most intensely plain;
He lost his ornamental half,
  Which I would have you gain.

Now here is brave advice, my boy,
  Which you will take, of course,
And if within a twelvemonth's time
  You don't admit its force,
Why, any Indiana judge
  Will grant you a divorce!

And if my arguments should fail
  To have convincing weight,
The succedaneum at the close
  May prove a tempting bait—
For with this legal safety-valve,
  A man may laugh at fate!

TAKE IT EASY.

ADMIT that I am slightly bald—
  Pray who's to blame for that?
And who is wiser for the fact
  Until I lift my hat?
Beneath the brim my barbered locks
  Fall in a careless way,
Wherein my watchful wife can spy
  No lurking threads of gray.

What though, to read compactest print,
  I'm forced to hold my book
A little farther off than when
  Life's first degree I took?
A yoke of slightly convex lens
  The needful aid bestows,
And you should see how wise I look
  With it astride my nose.

Don't talk of the infernal pangs
  That rheumatism brings—
I'm getting used to pains and aches,
  And all those sort of things.
And when the imp Sciatica
  Makes his malicious call,
I do not need an almanac
  To tell me it is Fall.

Besides, it gives one quite an air
  To travel with a cane,
And makes folk think you "well to do,"
  Although you are in pain.
A fashionable hat may crown
  Genteelest coat and vest,
But ah! the sturdy stick redeems
  And sobers all the rest.

A man deprived of natural sleep
  Becomes a stupid elf,
And only steals from father Time
  To stultify himself:
So if you'd be a jovial soul,
  And laugh at life's decline,
Take my advice—turn off the gas
  And go to bed at nine!

An easy cushioned rocking-chair
   Suits me uncommon well,
And so do liberal shoes—like these—
   With room for corns to swell;
I cotton to the soft lambs' wool
   That lines my gloves of kid,
And love elastic home-made socks—
   Indeed, I always did!

But what disturbs me more than all,
   Is that sarcastic boys
Prefer to have me somewhere else
   When they are at their noise;
That while I try to look and act
   As like them as I can,
They will persist in MISTER-ing me,
   And calling me a man!

HOLIDAY RHYMES.

THAT Christmas is coming we know from the wagons
  All laden with turkeys about the street corners;
From shows in shop windows of filagreed flagons,
  And plum cakes, so tempting to little Jack Horners.

From toys which the vendors display by the acre,
  From holiday books with their fanciful gilding;
By sleds all so fresh from the hands of the maker,
  By boys who are wild with their own castle-building.

Now carts from the country bring forests of branches,
  Of pine and of hemlock, that, woodsily fragrant,
At church doors are tumbled in green avalanches,
  And pilfered by many a juvenile vagrant.

Now housewives are busy with pungentest spices,
  With pumpkins, and pastry, and cakes full of raisins;
With crumpets and doughnuts of quaintest devices,
  And mince pies that Biddy so daintily "saysons."

Now Charley his skates all excitedly buckles,
   And, winged like a Mercury, rushes on danger,
While Grandpa alternately fidgets and chuckles,
   To see that the rogue to all fear is a stranger.

Yes, Christmas is coming! Just look at the bonnets—
   Those birds' nests entangled in rainbows and roses;
Whose owners' red cheeks would drive bards into sonnets,
   Were it not for the sight of their still redder noses.

That last line is shocking!—and quite out of keeping—
   And ought to be banished from Christmas society;
For while with delight youthful pulses are leaping,
   Our old ones should beat with the strictest propriety.

RHYMES FOR THE TIMES.

You tell me all breathe freely now—
   That we have seen the worst,
Because the gold has disappeared,
   And all the Banks have burst;
And that whereas a month ago
   Men trembled with affright,
They now assume serener looks,
   And times are coming "right."

An odd and antithetical
   Philosophy is this,
That twists your friends' financial woe
   To your financial bliss.
Our hopes thus tempt the tongue to strip
   Dilemma of its horns,
And thus our bleeding fingers clip
   The rosebud from its thorns.

It may be so.—I know I'm bound
  To think as others do,
And fain would I believe their words
  Are absolutely true.
The smoke and pudder overhead
  Perhaps have passed away,
But what mean all these sighs and moans,
  This pallor of dismay?

Ah, let me pause and think awhile—
  Is this the traveled road?
The highway for the human mind
  To reach its high abode?
Is gold the noblest aim of man,
  Or what the gold will bring?—
Come—go with me and hear the birds
  In yonder branches sing.

Yes, stroll with me through pastures green
  Where many a wild flower grows,
And tread on brakes that lend perfume
  To every breeze that blows.
Look through the grand old forest aisles
  Down which the sunlight shines,
And harken to their monotones,
  And smell the breath of pines.

Hark to the music of the brook,
　So full of soft delight;
And hear the wind-harp in the trees
　That charms the summer night.
Then lay your ear against the bark
　And hear the chestnuts grow,
And listen to the quivering leaves
　That whisper soft and low.

Look where the noble rivers run—
　The life-blood of the land!
That leave a blessing ere they kiss
　The ocean's belt of sand.
And mark the orchards, red with fruit,
　And see the gardens smile—
O feast your eyes with scenes like this,
　And be rejoiced the while.

It is indeed a goodly land,
　That meets your earnest gaze,
Inlaid with bearded fields of grain,
　And bright with golden maize.
And man is here with open brow,
　And strong in rudest health;
O where the heart is warm and true,
　There is a nation's wealth.

These pleasant scenes are yours and mine,
  Or may be if we choose;
And as the world is rosy hued,
  Don't tinge it with " the blues."
Thank God for health! Take heart again—
  The times will surely mend,
Though notes should go to protest still,
  And all the Banks suspend.

November, 1857.

ADVERTISEMENT.

I ALSO have a lot to sell,
  Whereon a State House might be placed;
A lot with ancient memories rife,
  And with some natural beauties graced.
A spot where antiquarian minds
  Cannot but love to delve and dig,
Whose soil is rich with unctuous juice
  That fills each green and growing twig.

Plough up the mould in early Spring—
  The self same odor meets you then,
As met the noses in old time
  Of our ancestral husbandmen.
Plant but a cabbage in the ground,
  And it will bourgeon just as fair
As the primeval cabbage did
  Which our forefathers planted there.

The suckers from the apple trees,
   That Parson Hooker sat beneath,
Are quite as vigorous as the old,
   And wear as brave a summer wreath:
Doubtless the vital sap that fills
   The hearts of those impressive trees,
Thrills to the voice from yonder Hall
   That loads this sudden patriot breeze.

And the same brook that sung its song
   In those revered and sainted days,
Still ripples o'er the shelving rocks,
   Still glistens in the morning's rays;
But, unlike other storied streams
   That lave full many a charming spot,
This stream has one especial charm—
   It runs beside *my* blessed lot!

Here the first christian puppy died
   That ever barked in Hartford town;
Here the first cat her litter dropped,
   That down the bank were cast to drown;
And here, as early records tell,
   Was born the first colonial calf,
Whose advent pleased the Parson so,
   It hindered half a paragraph.

18

Here the first loving couple came,
  With throbbing hearts and trembling hands,
For Parson H. to bind and weld,
  And join in wedlock's holy bands;
And here that same fond couple came
  To have their first-born boy baptized,
With water from the very stream
  That makes my lot so highly prized.

If patriot themes are wanted still,
  To raise the value of the lot,
I'll tell you how the train-bands once
  Marched boldly to the very spot;
And how, right in the front of it,
  They stopped to drill and exercise,
And beat the drum, and blow the fife,
  To witch the youngsters' ears and eyes.

It bears, indeed, a thousand charms,
  That I've no space to mention here,
Which cast a glow around, and make
  Its patriotic title clear.
And so, while priests and lawyers write,
  And pesky politicians plot,
This, after all, must prove to be,
  Among them all, the likeliest lot.

There's land enough—and not too much—
  Historic memories cluster round it;
The slope of ground is just the same,
  Or nearly, as our fathers found it;
It is a legendary nook,
  Where olden time has left its trace;
Where Parson Hooker lived and died—
  In short—I want to sell the place!

THE PARVENU

Ten years ago I knew him well—
    A sort of good-for-nothing fellow,
Who lounged about with roots to sell,
    And often got exceeding mellow;
A hanger-on about the skirts
    And shabby purlieus of society,
Who, guiltless of such things as shirts,
    Enjoyed a dubious notoriety.

Indeed, the man was very poor—
    And what was worse, extremely lazy;
A kind of trouble hard to cure,
    But such as rarely drives one crazy.
His wife was just his proper match,
    An idle gossip, and a slattern,
Whose frock, with time and frequent patch,
    Knew nevermore its native pattern.

They lived, as 'twere, from hand to mouth—
   She dawdling over pots and kettles;
He in a constant state of drouth,
   And both in frequent want of victuals.
Prophetic neighbors sagely said
   They were the fag-ends of creation,
And, from the vagrant life they led,
   The work-house was their destination.

But strange denouements will arise
   In this our reeling world of chances,
Which often cause as much surprise
   As those we read of in romances,
Where sometimes men of small account
   Become inflated, like a bladder,
And from the very bottom mount
   The topmost round of fortune's ladder.

It happened that our hero, then,
   While grubbing roots, or culling simples,
Discovered in some neighboring glen
   A prize that purpled all his pimples:
Some common weed, perhaps, that grew
   Among the sumachs or the teasels,
Which he declared would pain subdue,
   And even triumph over measles.

Compounding thence a salve, or pill,
    He advertised it in the papers,
A purge for every human ill—
    Consumption, cancer, gout, or vapors.
In short, it was a sovereign cure
    For all the aches that flesh is heir to,
So safe, so speedy, and so sure,
    That all the world its charms must swear to.

From New Orleans to Isle Pictou
    Its virtues blazed on post and pillar,
And many an ailing mortal knew
    The magic of the great pain-killer.
The wonders that it daily worked
    Were told in broad pictorial posters,
And cripples, who on crutches jerked,
    Exultant leaped, empiric boasters.

The world delights in being gulled,
    And loves a quack, and buys his nostrum,
And all suspicious thoughts are lulled
    Whene'er the juggler mounts his rostrum.
His pill or salve—no matter which—
    Baptized with some Greek name, or Latin,
Is bought by poor men, and by rich,
    By wives in rags, and maids in satin.

But now that same repulsive man,
   The once despised and shiftless sinner,
Lives only as a nabob can,
   Whose Tokay helps digest his dinner.
He owns a house of Portland stone,
   That fronts four city lots by measure,
And is to town and country known
   As blessed with fortune, fame, and leisure.

His portly form is daily seen
   In ornate coat and lustrous vesting,
While her balloon-like crinoline
   Is most immensely interesting.
And they who had no loving friend,
   Ten years ago, to aid or cheer them,
Have now a host, who freely spend
   Both time and cash to hover near them.

Their parties—they are perfect jams!
   And of entire respectability;
That is, a crowd of snobs and shams
   Endorse their own and his gentility.
The daily paper wildly swears
   The show surpasses scenes Elysian,
And paints the gaudy dress she wears
   With all a milliner's precision.

Wherever lady Fashion brings
  Her leaden sons and brazen daughters;
Where Newport seaward lifts its wings,
  Or Saratoga pours its waters,
They shed their patronizing rays
  On all the Joneses and Malonys—
The old man with his spanking grays,
  And Hopeful with his tandem ponies.

And she—beloved by parasites—
  Emerged from dirt and meagre diet,
Surrounded by her satellites,
  Without a train is never quiet:
Elate while her brave jewels blaze,
  And robed in silks of gorgeous pattern,
She shines in those reflected rays,
  As shines the star-girt planet Saturn.

I saw them in the surging crowd,
  Flushed with the giddy season's glory,
And as each head respectful bowed,
  I read the old familiar story;
The worm become a butterfly,
  Proud of his accidental riches,
The grub, transferred to Fashion's sky,
  From rags and more congenial ditches.

THOUGHTS

OVER A RAILROAD BOND.

IT is a very pretty thing,
  And charmingly engraved;
As neatly gotten up a cheat
  As ever broker shaved.
And I have quite a lot of them,
  All safe and snug at home,
Enough to make a picture book
  As large as Gibbon's Rome.

I thought I bought them very cheap,
  At only eighty-three.—
Indeed, we higgled quite a time
  Before we could agree;
"What! Eighty-three for ten per cents?
  Dear Sir, you must be crazed—
Yet, I shall have to let them go,
  For money must be raised."

19

Before that blessed week was out
　I smelt a sort of rat,
For I was told that I could buy
　For even less than that.
My neighbor bought for seventy-six,
　I never asked him how—
But I am far from sad to learn
　That he has got them now.

Those thousand dollar promises
　Are printed by the ream!
And being secured by mortgages
　How very safe they seem.
Moreover, I reserved the right
　To change them into shares,
Whose income by and by would be
　A fortune for my heirs.

The coupons—those delicious things!
　How temptingly they look;
As beautifully lithographed
　As Olney's copy-book.
Yes, there they are—not one cut off—
　The ranks are perfect yet,
And like to be, for all that I
　For them shall ever get.

The boy who shows for half a dime
   Six rattlesnakes alive,
Was urging me, the other day,
   To view his precious hive:
"I say, sir—want to see the snakes?
   One on 'em's eat a toad:—
I'll let you see 'em for a Bond
   Of that 'ere Western Road!"

Ah well—the dream is over now,
   And so I sit and sigh,
And curse the day when oily tongues
   Persuaded me to buy:
I spend my time with tearful eyes,
   O'er their delusive charms,
In singing sad lugubrious hymns
   And penitential psalms.

A BERKSHIRE BREEZE.

AND this is Berkshire! Broad and bright
The volume opens to my sight,
Valleys and lakes are at my feet,
And beaded brooks come down to meet,
With many a dash and arrowy bound,
   The calmer stream that shines below;
Fair stream, that having sweetly wound
Its loving arms the hills around,
   Lingers to clasp and keep them so.

I've seen full many an Autumn day,
   In many a bright October,
And mused beneath the foliage gay,
   And walked the hill sides sober;
But never, in my wanderings all,
Did my delighted vision fall

On lovelier scene than this!
Here, where the eye in roving, rests
On valleys and on mountain crests,
On hills all overpranked with trees,
On clouds that flush yon azure seas—
The purple clouds, whose folding gates
Seem openings to the world that waits—
 The world beyond of bliss.

Here, where the frost and sun have met,
 It seems as if some airy rover
Last evening's sundown had upset,
 And spilled its dyes the woods all over.
O Beauty is a mountain maid,
 And artist troops unseen attend her;
This is her autumn masquerade,
 And these her robes of regal splendor!

Nestling among these Berkshire hills,
 Peep out the pleasant homes of men,
Who, flying from the care that kills,
Are hither come to rest their quills—
 Knights of the rampant pen!
Yes, when the fragrant winds of June
Found all the mountain harps in tune;
When birds made vocal green-leaved bowers,
And wet their glistening wings in showers;

When the bright ploughshare turned the mould,
　　Whose effluent odor filled the air,
And traveling sheep from many a fold
　　Flecked the steep banks and pastures fair;
Then did these town-caged pilgrims yearn
　　To leave the city's brick defiles,
And from the noisome pavement turn
　　To bask in Nature's genial smiles.

And hither do they wend their way,
Primed for a long bright holiday;
Here, snug ensconced, and safe embowered
　　Among the old umbrageous trees,
Where sentient life is rosy-houred,
　　They court luxurious ease.
Perhaps they court, in idle dreams,
'Mid winding paths by lazy streams,
　　The half forgotten muse,
And give imagination play,
While fancy plumes her airy way
　　To bathe in heavenly dews.

Here comes, to rest his weary brain,
　　The overtasked Divine,
Hoping to find surcease of pain
　　Beneath the whispering pine.

He comes from probing saddened souls,
  From pondering his great Master's plan,
From dubious dreams of what controls
  That inconsistent creature, Man,
To read in Nature's open face
  The secrets that perplex all Art,
And feel the dews, the hopes, the grace
  That soothe the burdened heart.

The breeze, the streams, the trees, the flowers
Transport him back to childhood's hours,
And airy tones around him swim,
Sweet as his mother's cradle hymn.
He flies to sports, that, when a boy
Filled his elastic life with joy;
And seizing fishpole, line and hook,
With stealthy tread seeks out the brook;—
Impales, unmoved, a fellow-worm,
Sees it in tortuous writhings squirm,
Adroitly casts the hair-line out,
Stops—listens—jerks—and lo! a trout!

Thus day by day he beats the stream,
  'Till tired and sunburned—yet elate—
  He sees the season culminate,
And wakes from his delightful dream.
So having at his ease amassed
Sufficient health and strength to last
'Till winter's toilsome march be passed,

Takes one long breath his lungs to fill,
Repacks his Edwards on the Will,
   And back from whence he came;
There, in vexed waters never still,
Beneath the great tree Ygdrasil,
   To fish for nobler game.

And here's the summer haunt of him,
Whose fancy most delights to skim
   The glittering sea of fun;
A brimming, broad and liberal sea,
Before whose breezes, dancing free,
   His shallop loves to run.
That light barque never comes to shore
Without a freight of precious ore;
For pregnant is the bellying sail,
And perfumed is the favoring gale
   That bends the taper mast;
And when his pennant points to land,
Impatient listeners crowd the strand,
   Awaiting HOLMES' last!

And this long promised son of song,
For whom the world has waited long,
Though baptized in Castalia's dews,
Stands lightly toying with the muse.
He, to his own intense delight,
Provokes our whetted appetite,

With intellectual whips and creams,
And such like after-dinner themes;
Gives us the play hours of his wits,
In tantalizing crumbs and bits;
Just lifts the screen, that we may guess
What hoards of wealth behind it press,
'Till, though rebellious midriffs ache,
And non-resistant muscles break,
Yet, with our nerves relaxed and sore,
Like Dickens' boy we cry for MORE!

Let pedants, if they will, condemn
The luscious fruit, too rich for them,
  For jaundiced eyes too fair,
But should they peel the velvet rind,
And squeeze the juicy pulp, they'd find
  The seeds of wisdom there.

Sworn foe to humbug and to cant,
He rips the windy bags of rant;
Strips from conceit the lion's skin,
And lets the tell-tale sunlight in,
  On empty heads to shine.
His wretched victims writhe and quail,
With inward pangs and visage pale,
As if the wag had dipped his pen
In some unsavory albumen,
  Or antimonial wine!

20

And when he tunes his harp to Spring,
  How clear the liquid notes!
The birds rush by on whistling wing,
  And soft the choral music floats.
Beneath his footsteps crush the flowers—
The lordly elm above him towers;
The maple buds in clusters fair
Hang trembling garlands in the air,
And the lithe birch its tassels swings,
Witched by the west wind's winnowing wings.

The hyacinth and daffodil
Their perfume through his verse distill;
Among his leaves a dainty group
Of lilies of the valley droop;
The fragile fern its fingers spreads,
Pale mountain daisies lift their heads,
The snow-drop turns its sweet lips up,
The tulip flaunts its gaudy cup;
The purple lilac's fragrance comes
To wile the bees from winter homes;
The mayflower wakes with Easter tides,
And like a wood-nymph coyly hides;
The cowslip from its velvet bed
Just lifts its unpretending head;
The honeysuckle flings perfume
Above where purple violets bloom,
And golden buttercups uplift
A chalice for night's dewy gift.

One need not seek the warming fields
  To watch the early blossoms grow,
His page the same aroma yields,
  And there you feel them bud and blow.
His floral groves and rustling trees
"Smell of the woods and morning breeze,"
And, cheated by the bright ideal
  The wondrous minstrel's flinging o'er you,
His prismy sketches all seem real,
  And Spring's embroidery lies before you.

And in his thoughtful, pithy lines
The welcome news transparent shines,
  "This is the coming man!"
One single phrase admits the fact,
That half his powers are held intact,
When, as to pose us puzzled wights,
He tells us that he never writes
  So funny as he can!

Considerate bard! to spare the lives
Of us and of our precious wives,
By keeping on an even poise
The valve that stops explosive noise.—
But ah! if through a sad mistake,
  In some unguarded hour,
He should omit to watch the brake,
What awful work the slip would make,
  What wrecks proclaim his power!

Buttons would fly, and waistbands burst—
  Men tumble in convulsions dire,
While wailing infants, halfway nursed,
Would shriek to see, prone in the dust,
  Their mothers and their hopes expire;
Strong featured men would find their jaws
  Expanded, like a rose full blown,
And, chuckling o'er the exciting cause,
  Forget amid their pains to groan.
In droves they would go wild and die,
And piled along the pathway lie,
  Like suicidal gnomes;
And "crowners' juries" all would find,
In most irreverent frame of mind,
  "Died from excess of HOLMES!"

LINES,

WRITTEN FOR THE CENTENNIAL CELEBRATION AT WOODBURY.

MYSTERIOUS notes were abroad on the air—
Significant hints of some weighty affair:
Rumors increased 'till they rose to a shout,
And now we all see what the stir was about.

Ye modest admirers, who've nothing to say,
Make room! for spread-eagle is coming this way.
We stand, as it were, in our forefathers' shoes,
And the time for tall talking's too precious to lose.

Here frolicksome age shall grow young at the core,
And youth shall strike hands with the boys of threescore;
Brim full of good feeling—O call it not folly—
We've assembled on purpose to laugh and be jolly.

Ye attornies—turn over a holiday leaf;
The facts are before you—and here is the brief!
So give us as much as you please of your jaw,
But don't, if you love us, don't let it be law.

Ye grave Boanerges—who thunder at sin,
Let your features relax to a good natured grin;
Pretermit theological chaffing and chat,
And talk about buttercups, birds, and all that.

Forget, O my friends, in this glorified hour,
The Parson who vanquished that dreadful pow-wow-er;
But remember the Backus and Bellamy jokes,
And up and be merry like rational folks.

Sink the shop, O ye trader in dry goods, to-day—
Just look at the prospect right over the way;
Don't the sight of the Pomperaug hills and green valleys
Beat all your gay patterns on muslins and challies?

Ye medical men—whose dreams are of drugs,
Omit for a while your professional shrugs;
Give the go-by to boluses, blisters, and nux,
And think of the dandelions, daisies and ducks.

Ye farmers—the nearest to Nature's own breast,
Who draw from her stores what her children love best;
Who irradiate towns with fresh butter and cheese,
And tickle our palates with lamb and green peas;

I remember your haymows so fragrant in June;
Your pumpkins, as large and as round as the moon;
The green corn we roasted and ate on the sly,
And the rye'n'ndian bread, and the—Oh! let us cry!

It makes my mouth water to talk of such things.—
The truth is, you farmers are Nature's own kings;
And the queens! would you see the true test of *their* worth?
Just look at those boys! Aren't they proud of their birth!

Of course, we'll remember, and speak of with pride,
Seth Warner, and others who fought by his side;
And grand Ethan Allen—the hero all over—
Who conquered Fort Ti. in the name of Jehovah!

Historians assert that you'd only one witch—
But history makes an unfortunate hitch,
For witches still flourish—as witness these groups!
Though for halters and faggots you substitute hoops.

Then a health to old Woodbury—merry or grave—
And long in the land may her progeny wave,
Nor forget where their excellent grandmothers sleep,
While their own little babies are learning to creep.

LINES,

READ TO THE PUTNAM PHALANX, AT BOSTON.

(After dinner.)

It's just what I expected, and I cannot well complain.—
Because a fellow did it once you thought he would again;
And so, to meet the challenger in case one should appear,
I brought a loaded gun along:—you see I have it here!

———

I was busy with a customer about a little bill,
With one eye on his pocket-book and one upon the till:
The gross amount was figured up—it wasn't very large—
And he had raised his battle cry, of "charge, Chester, charge!"

When steps me in a portly man, who couldn't see his knee,
With a smile upon his lip, and said "I want you Mr. C."
I knew he was no constable—those caitiffs seldom smile—
And thus with words of blandishment my ear he did beguile.

"Our Phalanx, whose ambition soars beyond a prosy drill,
Is going on a Pilgrimage to famous Bunker Hill;
We mean to stand, with hat in hand, where glorious Putnam fought,
And tread the soil where noble deeds by him were nobly wrought.

We go with no inflamed desire, nor any sly intent
To bring away by force of arms the Charlestown monument:—
Although it were an easy thing to do so if we chose,
As every body who has seen the stalwart Phalanx knows.

And we want you to come along. We'll have a jovial time—
And don't forget to bring with you a pleasant bit of rhyme.
The day is fixed for Tuesday next—no dodging for the rain—
And pray be prompt, because, you see, we're going on a train!"

Well, here I am—a little man among top-booted screamers—
Like to a clipper 'mid a fleet of huge Great Eastern steamers:
A sort of rakish letter o'marque, beside my big compeers,
So let my signals all be marked as meant for private ears.

I'm told your mothers know you're out—how is it with your wives?
And have the thoughtful creatures got insurance on your lives?
I trust when you are safely back they'll ask no idle questions,
To answer which would interfere with delicate digestions.

It has been sometimes asked of me, in quite a serious way,
If you in case of actual war would mingle in the fray?
I answer, yes: and what is more, no danger would you shun,
For it is quite impossible that such great men should run!

21

No—be assured of this one thing, though large the target be,
You'd let a broadside rake your ranks ere one of you would flee:
Cocked hats might wilt, and breeches rip, and coats be rent and torn,
Yet still amid the thickest fight your banner would be borne.

Look at the standard bearer there and doubt it if you can!
And think if those odd legs would save our excellent Squire Mann!
And Deming too—the enemy would make a deadly breach
In every thing his broadcloth hid ere he the rear could reach.

The mental courage that dilates each soldier's flashing eye,
Would be excited by the fact that he must do or die.
So all ye bull-necked Britishers beware these men of might—
They wont surrender, cannot run—but, glory! how they'll fight!

You may talk about Thermopylæs and Marathons of old;
Of Lodi and of Waterloo, and all their heroes bold;
I'll bet a score of pumpkin pies, and help the party eat 'em,
That Major Goodwin and his troop would give 'em odds and beat 'em!

You've one might rank, if so he chose, with old Demosthenes:
And a lineal son of that old Greek we call Thucydides:
And others who but bide their time to show their fellow men
That they can wield, as Cæsar did, the sword as well as pen.

One member may his patients purge, and one may shove the plane,
And one may have an oily tongue and wag the same for gain;
You may have merchants, presidents, and men from toil retired,
But all with warlike visions now are most intensely fired.

Your Colt would shoot a dozen foes, the while the rest were aiming:
And Ashmead's hammer, like old Thor's, the cohorts would be maiming:
And Tiffany, if duty called, would prove no terrapin,
But like a valiant printer send a frequent bullet in.

And where, in case of a retreat, would neighbor Strong be found?
Dead—or like Falstaff feigning death—along the bloody ground.
And Sharp would never mount the box with four-in-hand again,
But like a hunted buffalo loom up among the slain.

Well, let us hope there'll be no war—we're quiet-loving folk—
And really, after all that's said, this fighting is no joke.
I never liked the trade, myself, since I was quite a lad,
When Billy Wolcott broke my head, and pommelled me so bad!

We've come to visit Bunker Hill. We've also come to dine.
Moreover, we're to taste a glass of Boston people's wine.
(I wonder if they would have thrown such nectar in the sea,
If George had taxed it as he did that plaguy lot of tea!)

What good things they to-day provide, to-day let us discuss—
For when another morning breaks they'll breakfast upon us!
To-morrow they will surely have, (dressed up as latest news,)
A dish of Putnam Phalanx served, to flank their prandial stews.

Ah! bless those editorial chaps:—its a way they've got,
Of seizing jokes, like buckwheat cakes, while they are piping hot;
And while the jokers are abed and dreaming of new feats,
Those typos will be "setting up"—and pulling off the sheets!

May you look back upon this day with patriotic pride,
And with a keener relish still your ambling hobby ride;
And may those solemn looking hats acquire no rakish tricks,
Nor ever be a lurking place for sad convivial bricks.

LINES,

ON THE PRESENTATION OF A WREATH TO THE COMMANDER
OF THE PHALANX, BY A GRANDDAUGHTER
OF GENERAL PUTNAM.

FLOWERS from his grave—and by his Grandchild brought!
  What emblems more could sanctify the scene?
With tender memories each soul was fraught,
  Evoked by her who bore that garland green.
Strong men forgot their boasted manhood then,
  And eyes that seldom wept with tears were dim.—
In war's grim guise her Grandsire conquered men,
  She, with these frail memorials of him.

Was not his shadowy presence near her there,
  The while she plucked those leaves and blossoms wild?
And did not seraphs, hovering in the air,
  Pronounce a benediction on the child?
They surely did;—for, still unseen, but seeing,
  The air was rife with their sustaining power,
And, all intensified, her sentient being
  Communed with his in that most holy hour.

THE VOYAGE.

A BALLAD.

'Tis now an hundred years or more, since on an Autumn day
A little fleet from Hartford shores got slowly under way;
A little fleet indeed it was—two schooners and a scow,
And one batteau that led the van with its imposing prow.

Brave were the hearts of those who manned the enterprising craft,
Men who had served apprenticeship on flat-boat and on raft;
And well they knew all weather signs, and when to beat or scud,
And every hidden sand-bar knew, and every reef of mud.

And as they rounded old Dutch Point that juts so broad and sheer,
They gaily swung their hats aloft and gave a hearty cheer;
The favoring breezes bore them on and filled each bellying sail,
Until the fleet careened before the keel-compelling gale.

Then firmly every hard glazed hat was on each forehead pressed,
And tightened every strap that girt each linsey-woolsey vest;
Firm was the helm within the grasp, and bright the look-out kept,
As bravely o'er the treacherous bars the stately squadron swept.

The mouth of Salmon Brook is passed, witch haunted though it be,
And starboard shines the sedgy "Cove," a tranquil summer sea;
And now the odoriferous gales from Wethersfield are met,
That with a pungent moisture make their tingling eyelids wet.

"Sabean odors" freight the breeze that follows from the strand,
While with reluctant nose they leave the aromatic land;
And as across the rail he leans, each skipper heaves a sigh,
And wipes the sympathetic tear that trembles in his eye.

Now Glastenbury looms in sight—there where the turbid flood
Sweeps round the swallow-punctured banks and soaks the yellow mud;
And there it was the angry wind came freshening from the west,
And sent the curling waves along the river's troubled breast.

What ho! bold seaman.—Lift your eyes above the creaking mast!
The clouds are hurrying dark and wild, the scud is driving fast;
The gulls are screaming in the air, the waves are black below,
And the foam beneath your keel is in a phosphorescent glow.

"Hard up the helm and shorten sail!" the Captain's voice rings clear,
"The convoy is—I don't know where, in this here atmosphere;
There is no gleam of blessed light to break the darkness now—
Our comrade is clean out of sight, and where's the gallant scow!"

The gloomy clouds, the roaring winds, the thick and blinding spray
Sent pallor to the swarthy brows of stalwart men that day;
And up and down the river broad the fleet were scattered wide,
Breasting the storm as best they might, withouten chart or guide.

Ah! me—it was a fearsome time: stout hearts were full of dread—
A dangerous shore beneath their lee, the storm-king overhead!
O then it was that pale dismay sat on their tell-tale looks,
As they thought of "bloudy salvages," of Moodus, and of spooks!

And there were sounds of starting pumps, of ropes and timbers riven,
And all that sort of din which fills a ship by tempest driven;
The men all swore they never knew the waves to run so wild,
Nor never knew, in all their lives, the river so much r'iled.

'Twere vain to tell of spars that split while they were sadly tossed,
Of pails and hatches knocked about, and oars and thole-pins lost;
Nor O! how dreary passed the night with each bewildered crew,
While landmarks, and the land itself were hidden from their view.

But when the sun shone out once more, and weary winds were still,
And they found themselves right off against the bluffs of Rocky Hill,
The sight of pine trees waving o'er the beetling ledges bold,
Was a most precious sight to those poor sailors wet and cold.

And then the haggard skippers joined once more in counsel sweet,
And told to each the dangers wild that had beset the fleet.—
One's keel had grazed upon a bar, one lost his grappling hook,
And one had run afoul a stump, and one—had seen a spook!

It was the captain of the scow, the frightful spook that saw—
And awful form, amid the storm, with grim and bloody jaw;
And it had two great burning eyes within its horrid head,
And raven wings that thrice it flapped before it shrieked and fled.

With anxious fears those mariners then spread each time-worn sail,
And one on other trembling gazed, with quivering lips and pale,
The very wind itself was awed, and did forget to blow,
And so, while riding out the calm, they all went down below.

But wind and men got o'er their fright, and both came up at length,
The breeze to plume its drooping wing, the men to show their strength;
And so at last they bore away adown the tranquil stream,
Between the green and sloping banks, as in a pleasant dream.

Help, ho!" A sharp and sudden cry: a surge—a crash—a shock:
Help or we sink—the plaguy scow has struck upon a rock!"
Alarm filled every seaman's soul and sat on every brow,
For sure it seemed the surging waves would overwhelm the scow.

But ere a hand could reach the boat or offer it an oar,
The treacherous rock, submerged, arose, and paddled to the shore!
With wonder great they did behold the cause of the mishap,
Which proved to be a turtle there indulging in a nap!

The steering oar again is bent—again they hold their way,
The white foam flying from their keels, and from their brows the spray;
Fair Upper Houses now are passed, and Middletown in sight,
And every nerve is strained to reach their port before the night.

All in good time the fleet was moored, wet jackets taken off,
And rattling fell the heavy sails as they swung to the wharf;
But where those jovial sailors went, when all was right and tight,
'Twere not well for me to tell, nor how they spent the night.

But it is true as gospel words, that on next Sunday morn,
When worshippers were called to prayer by the familiar horn,
Those men all came to render thanks, and pray with serious lips,
For those who traffic on the deep, and who go down in ships!

THE REPULSE.

A BALLAD.

In sixteen hundred ninety-three,
  The Charter of our embryo State
Was deemed a broad protective shield,
  As potent as a bond of fate.
It bore a front, the like of which
  No proud crusader's ever knew,
Where desperate blows from haughty foes
  Fell harmless as the summer dew.

The king, though claiming right divine,
  Must yet succumb to public will;
He might be strong, but still would find
  That chartered rights were stronger still.
Wherefore the stern high-minded men
  Who laid fair freedom's corner-stone,
Were prompt to peril limb and life
  Against encroachments from the throne.

So when the royal Duke of York
  His pompous emissary sent,
To take command of all our troops,
  And thus the Charter circumvent,
That parchment shield was found to wield
  A power no duke could set aside,
Which never bent to Parliament,
  And no proud king could override.

This fact caused young Connecticut
  To battle stoutly for her rights;—
And when tall Colonel Fletcher came
  He saw some unexpected sights.
Our notions did not square with his,
  Which caused an internecine war,
That ended only with the flight
  Of this ill-starred embassador.

And yet, pursuant to his wish,
  The men were mustered under arms;
And stalwart troops they were to see,
  With sturdy limbs and horny palms.
Their Captain, Wadsworth, was a man
  Of slender build and modest mien,
But who a loftier spirit bore
  Than many a belted knight, I ween.

The line was formed. And Bayard then
  In voice sonorous, loud and clear,
Began:—but ere a page was read
  No word could any listener hear.
"Beat drums!" the irate Captain cried,
  And drum it was with right good will,
Until one might as well have tried
  To harken in a fulling mill.

"Silence!" the Colonel thundered forth—
  And straight the drummers ceased to play,
'Till Bayard raised his voice again,
  When Wadsworth shouted "Drum, I say!"
"Silence, you rebels!" shrieked the chief—
  The dauntless Captain answered "Drum!"
And drumsticks flew 'till Fletcher stopped,
  And then the sheepskin too was dumb.

The little Captain's spunk was up—
  While Fletcher's face grew red with rage,
To find his Aid was baffled thus
  In reading the initial page.
"Stand back!" the fearless soldier cried,
  As Fletcher glared with looks of fury—
"Another word, and this good sword,
  By Jove! shall let the daylight through ye!"

He *did* stand back—and, hot with wrath,
  Turned on his heel to quit the ground;
For well he wot the Captain's words
  Were something more than empty sound.
His cocked hat in the distance loomed,
  His angry voice sank low and lower,
Until his coat-tails disappeared
  Behind the neighboring tavern door.

And thus the chief who warrant held
  From one who Royal Duke was dubbed,
In presence of a Yankee crowd
  Was most incontinently snubbed.
Discomfited he stalked away,
  Pursued by much derisive laughter,
And harbored in his ear a flea
  Of largest size, forever after.

In gallant trim the troops moved on,
  With lofty step, to Court-House Square,
Where Captain Wadsworth made a speech
  That stirred each soldier's heart and hair.
Then with three cheers for chartered rights,
  And three for their unsullied flag,
They filed away, as fife and drum
  Struck up the vigorous "double drag."

The heirs of that determined band,
   Our Governor's Guards, are living yet,
And the same spirit nerves their arms
   That nerved the men whom Fletcher met;
Bear witness each Election day,
   When those tight-gaitered legs we see
March to the tune their fathers marched
   In sixteen hundred ninety-three!

THE TORY.

A BALLAD.

In seventeen hundred seventy-five,
  In one of fair New England's towns,
A rabid Tory lurked about,
  Regardless of his neighbors' frowns.
Repeated threats had no effect
  To drive him off or change his views,
And so the kind persuasive whigs
  Determined to apply the screws.

The Yankees of those troublous times
  When once resolved were very stern,
And tories found at last that they
  Had some sharp lessons yet to learn.
The king might rule beyond the sea—
  But only whigs could comprehend
That here, upon our Pilgrim soil,
  His reign was surely doomed to end.

And so this man at length was brought
　　To answer for his flagrant crime;
And there he swore that George the Third
　　Should be his king till end of time.
"You must recant," the judge exclaimed,
　　"Or else from yonder tree you swing."—
"Swing and be damned!" the tory cried,
　　"I will be loyal to my king."

"Not in our town," the boys replied—
　　So o'er his head a noose was slipped,
And round the emblematic pole
　　The ticklish rope was deftly whipped.
And then they ran the sinner up
　　To dangle in the air awhile—
And all with most artistic grace,
　　Quite in experienced hangman style.

A gallows is a pokerish thing,
　　However well or rudely built,
In sight of which, though brave and bold,
　　The shuddering wretch is like to wilt.
Indeed, I think it must have been
　　A shrewd invention of old Nick's,
To serve as a suspension bridge
　　For rogues to cross the river Styx.

But our unlucky hero thought
  This trap would hardly catch him yet,
And that his neighbors would not dare
  To carry out their monstrous threat.
Thus he made light of their demand,
  And scouted at the whole affair,
As being—what indeed it proved—
  A frolic, that would end in air!

While hoisting him on high, they cried
  "Shout LIBERTY, and you may go."
The fellow shook his stubborn head,
  And, as he landed, bellowed "No!"
Again they ran him up aloft
  To dance his second airy jig,
Like to a warning beacon set
  For any present lukewarm whig.

The same result. No rope, he said,
  The freedom of his will should bind;
His loyalty was firm and true,
  As whig committees now would find.
Once more the victim rose in air,
  When things assumed a serious look;
For now they let the caitiff swing
  Until he gurgled like a brook.

"Let go!" and down the subject fell,
  With features of a livid hue;
His bravery was oozing out
  From every pore his body knew.
And then he feebly swung his hat,
  Renounced the king in rueful tones,
Gave a faint cry for Liberty,
  And then subsided into groans.

At length the wretch recovered breath—
  And with lugubrious look of woe,
He thus in mournful accents spoke
  To those who had abused him so:
"You have the oddest sort of way
  In making whigs, if you but knew it;
But odd and cruel as it is,
  O gentlemen, it's sure to do it!"

Here was a case where coats of tar
  And feathers would have failed to act—
A case requiring skill and nerve,
  As well as a peculiar tact;
But well these Sons of Liberty
  Their special business understood,
And did it in a way that showed
  The temper of the neighborhood.

And thus this unregenerate man
  New light upon the subject got,
And found himself transmogrified
  From Royalist to Patriot.
Those stirring boys would not permit
  A tory wasp about their hive—
And that's the way they managed things
  In seventeen hundred seventy-five.

SACK AND SUGAR.

A BALLAD.

In seventeen hundred seventy-seven,
  When blows were dealt for life and land,
Fair women mingled in the fray,
  And lent at times a helping hand.
An instance floats before me now,
  Evolved from memory's smouldering heap,
That once beguiled my youthful ears,
  And lulled my drooping eyes to sleep.

East Hartford—famed for little else
  Than sand and watermelons now—
Was marked, in those brave times of old,
  By quite an enterprising row.
What time King George's red-coat force
  Strode o'er the land with bloody trail,
The sack and pillage happed, which now
  Becomes the staple of my tale.

Tea, sugar, rum, and other stores,
   In those rough days, were scarce and dear,
And folk resorted for supplies
   To measures that were somewhat queer.
Thus, once in Master Pitkin's store,
   All hid away from common view,
Were sundry casks of sugar stowed,
   Intended for the soldier crew.

The women—bless their patriot souls!—
   The whispered news indignant heard,
And straight resolved that not an ounce
   In British teacups should be stirred.
The tumult in their throbbing hearts
   Made every rounded bosom swell,
And caused delighted swains to flush,
   As muslin tuckers rose and fell.

Through all the region round about
   The spirit of adventure swept;
Girls talked of feats of arms by day,
   And dreamed of sugar when they slept.
A rendezvous at length is fixed,
   And Lyon's tavern is the spot,
Where troops throng in from Salmon Brook,
   From Podunk, and from Pewterpot.

And so, that August afternoon,
   To air-borne cries of *Katydid*,
Some two score damsels marched away
   For where the tempting prize was hid.
No flouting banner mocked the foe,
   No martial music shrieked "we come!"
For petticoats were flag enough,
   And quite superfluous fife and drum.

Poor badgered Pitkin—(tory he—
   Custodian of the precious stock,)
Grew pale, as any tory might,
   To meet this energetic flock.
With skirts tucked up through pocket holes,
   And arms akimbo, on they came,
Resolved, in dauntless maidenhood,
   To strike for sugar, and for fame!

Aghast the trembling sinner stood,
   And quailed before the potent power:—
Confronted by a crowd like this
   His craven spirit well might cower.
Besides—the band was flanked by three
   Tall sturdy chaps who knew the plan,
And so, like valiant Falstaff, he
   Turned tail at once and fairly ran.

Elated now, the victors ramped,
  And topsy-turvy turned the things;
Searched his dried-apple lofts and bins,
  And stripped his onions from the strings:
Ripped portly bags of feathers loose,
  Upset the kettles, pots, and pans,
And when they forced the cellar door
  Each female kick was like a man's!

At last, all snugly packed away,
  They found the luscious prize they sought;
Then promptly seized a neighboring cart,
  And two recumbent oxen caught.
The casks were safely rolled aboard,
  The excited captain shouted "Go!"
And off in triumph thus they bore
  The plunder from the routed foe.

Now, where that captured sugar went,
  No mortal ear was ever told;
But my opinion is, that all
  Beneath true Yankee tongues was rolled:
And that, indeed, about those days,
  When lovers' lips impulsive met,
The secret must have been betrayed,
  That it was somewhere handy yet!

Women had nerve and mettle then,
　　And proved their pluck and prowess too.—
This sketch, suggestive, merely hints
　　At deeds they were prepared to do.
They hated red-coats.—And they knew
　　That tories stood small chance for heaven,
Who prowled about Connecticut
　　In seventeen hundred seventy-seven!

24

NIP AND TUCK.

A BALLAD.

'TWAS on a bright October day,
   When every crimson leaf was still,
That Gibson took an early walk
   Along the brow of Staddle Hill.
The chattering chipmunk hears his step,
   With tail erect and eager ears,
While master woodchuck, waddling off,
   Straight for his distant burrow steers.

Now Gibson was a brawny man,
   Of lofty port and mighty limb,
And all the country wrestlers stood
   In reverential awe of him.
The famed Athlete could boast no form
   Of nobler mould, in olden days,
Than our good friend, whose ponderous strength,
   Belied his gentle thoughts and ways.

And as in meditative mood
  He wandered on his forest way,
Behold a bear's neglected cub
  Right in the open pathway lay.—
To see if its wild dam were near
  One searching glance he cast around,
Then cried "a prize!" and lightly raised
  The struggling vagrant from the ground.

The cub across his shoulder flung,
  He started off with rapid stride,
Mistrustful that the young one's cries
  Might bring its mother to his side.
And so they did. For Bruin heard,
  And leaping to the fierce attack,
Cried out, as plain as bear could cry,
  "You rascal, bring my baby back!"

But deuce a bit for that cared he.—
  So straightway starting on a run,
He cursed the brute, and inly wished
  That he had brought along his gun.
Now for a race! The man's ahead,
  But Bruin gains at every bound—
Four legs are more than match for two,
  And Gibson's plainly losing ground.

One desperate leap and Bruin's teeth
    The robber's linsey-woolsey tore;
The nip was close, but only urged
    The wounded man to run the more.
Another spring—when Gibson dodged
    Behind a hemlock, neat and clever,
But all too late—for Bruin's grip
    Had spoiled his pantaloons forever!

Down went the cub—and Gibson turned,
    With rearward smart, to face the foe,
And hand to foot they had it now,
    With hug for hug, and blow for blow.
But, quite accomplished in the art
    To scientific wrestlers known,
The man displayed most skill, and soon
    His brute antagonist was "thrown."

But neither one was freed as yet
    From that uncomfortable hug,
And Bear, defiant, gnashed his teeth,
    While Gibson cursed her ugly mug.
To both the grim embrace was like
    The anaconda's crushing fold,
As o'er the bank and down the hill
    The desperate couple, fighting, rolled.

The snapping twigs, the rattling stones,
　The clouds of dust betrayed their track,
Until the two, with sudden jolt,
　Brought up against a hackmatack.
With one accord they loosed the hold
　That bound them in this social tie,
And sadly blown, and bruised, and banged,
　Each turned and bid his foe good-by.

'Twas a drawn game—and victory raised
　No flag when the encounter ceased;
But that rough tussle was enough
　To satisfy both man and beast.
And thus came off this raciest
　Of all impromptu rigadoons,
Where Bruin lost her precious cub,
　As Gibson did his pantaloons!

BALLAD.

A BARON bold, on an iron-gray steed,
   Rode forth at the break of day,
Whose grim cadaverous looks were enough
   To fill one with dismay.

Over the level sward he rode,
   And over the moorland drear,
'Till reining his steed by the good green wood,
   He fiercely paused to hear.

He plunged his spurs in the horse's flanks,
   And the horse plunged into the wood,
And the forest rang to his dreadful shout,
   As an orderly forest should.

Before the rage of that Baron bold
   The strongest nerves might shrink,
For his natural ire was doubled that day
   By a double allowance of drink!

And as he flourished his naked sword
  And dared his foe to the fight,
There issued forth from another wood
  Another powerful knight:

A knight on a snorting red-roan steed,
  With a longer sword than the first,
Who, out of his own particular wood,
  Like a wild tornado burst.

In about a quarter of an hour, or so,
  Their blades were dripping wet,
And the blood ran down, as it always runs,
  When two such fiends are met.

'Twas a horrible sight to see the fight,
  As the sparks from their armor flew,
And a matter of doubt as to which of the knights
  Was the drunkest man of the two.

The stalwart blows fell thick and fast,
  And the trampled grass grew red,
Until, with a trenchant crashing blow,
  Each split the other's head!

And then, with a dull and leaden sound,
  They both like plummets dropped,
And the riderless horses ran away,
  And probably never have stopped.

And who those grisly foemen were,
  No mortal man could tell;
For all unburied they were left
  On the wet leaves where they fell.

The wolves and the crows had a grand carouse,
  And noisily ate their fill;
But the scattered bones, and the grinning skulls
  On the sward are bleaching still.

THE GARDENER.

PEEP through the palings of your neighbor's fence,
Kept sound and bright regardless of expense,
And there behold the new-fledged gardener stand,
Sole owner of those few clean rods of land.
A city bud, just bursting into bloom,
Who, as he prospers, wants more elbow-room:
Who, by much saving, and some lucky hits,
Is rich enough to wish to air his wits.
He leaves the ledger and its irksome toil,
To make a day-book of his garden soil;
Warmed by the rays prosperity has lent,
His aspirations here have found a vent;
And as the tulip feels Spring's subtle power,
So this dry bulb has burst into a flower;
Charmed with the sweet employment, he can feel
All a new convert's pardonable zeal.
Look how he lords it over honest Pat—
"Trim me this pear tree, and transplant me that;

25

Put this peony in the centre bed;
Dig up this weed, and plant a rose instead."
Poor Pat, obsequious, works with all his might,
'Till soon, between them, Chaos looms in sight.

The dear man's lessons have but just begun,
Although he rates himself A, No. 1,
Full of good feeling, he accounts it *prime*,
In such fine grounds to spend his leisure time.

Our novice knows, beginner though he be,
The learned name for every shrub and tree;
That is, he harbors such a kind of whim,
But leans on labels that adorn each limb;
Talks learnedly of fall and winter fruits,
And what manures are 'counted best for roots;
Can tell the odds, like Affleck, or like Prince,
Between an apple and an apple-quince;
Knows which the dwarf, and which the standard trees,
And says they came from far beyond the seas;
Knows they are genuine, knows each seedling "true,"
Because he had them from a man he knew.
Which means, he bought them (paid the money down)
From a French gentleman, who passed through town;
And who assured him, with sinister glance,
That he brought every tree, himself, from France;
That though impostors, cheats, were all about,
Yet one was sure to find the rascals out!

Good easy man—he's not the first who's made,
In roses or in fruits, this kind of trade,
And not, I fear, the last one on the list
Who'll deem French morals have an ugly twist:—
For Frenchmen's consciences seem supple things,
When cheating Yankees, or dethroning kings.

Still our green gardener carols on his way,
Well pleased with this new hobby-horse to play;
Borrows pet phrases from poor Downing's work,
About the aphis and the little Turk,
Winter-kill, fire-blight, apple-borer grim,
Root grafting, mulching, pruning-in a limb:—
These artist phrases ripple from his tongue
As if he'd been indoctrinated young.

And yet, he's learned so much that he can tell,
By the young buds, if things are doing well;
Knows at a glance a sucker from a shoot,
And guesses shrewdly at the sorts of fruit;
He knows a cherry from a Bartlett pear,
Is sure next year his peaches all will bear;
Has learned that sunshine does a deal of good
In opening blossoms and in ripening wood;
Is taught to let his flower-pots all remain
Quite unprotected from the summer rain;
Knows a day-lily from a buttercup,
Knows both will thrive—if planted right end up!

And yet, for all he is so wondrous wise,
Puts faith in all that florists advertise!
Takes the whole tribe of horticultural prints,
And pins his faith upon their monthly hints;
Takes their advice to use a hoe or spade,
And seems, poor tyro, tenderly afraid
To cut a dandelion, until he's seen
The exact direction in his magazine.

Ah, there it is! That blessed floral guide
Is, like his trowel, ever at his side;
He's all impatience for the day that brings
The last smooth number, full of pictured things,
Which tells him when to plant, and when to mulch,
And is to him a Californian gulch;—
Grateful to him, as to his grass the dews,
And O! so full of horticultural news!

THE REASON WHY.

TO F. S. C.

You wonder why my playful muse
　　Has been so coy of late—
As if impulsive Pegasus
　　Should never stop to "bait!"
Besides—while rhymes are blossoming
　　One's hopes may run to seed,
And so I pause in my career,
　　And drop the lines—to feed!

Two sides there are to human life—
　　The dreamy one I've tried,
And now I tread with sturdier step
　　The bread-and-butter side.
Along the paths of Merchandise
　　My cautious way I feel,
And deal in Iron bars for gain,
　　And sometimes even—steel!

Repress your rising smile, O friend,
  Nor spoil my bit of fun;
A metal pen may be allowed
  A sympathetic pun.
And since I've put with madam Trade
  My faculties to nurse,
Thought bourgeons, and o'erruns the bounds
  And paths of sober verse.

Yet "quips and cranks" that once were rife,
  Grow scarcer on my lips;
The light that hovered o'er my pen
  Has suffered an eclipse:
I wear an unobtrusive hat,
  A Linkinwater coat,
And memories of departed gloss
  Around my waistcoat float.

Folk speak of me as a sedate
  And proper kind of man,
And overlook my youthful freaks—
  Or try to, all they can:
Indeed, I more than half suspect
  It *was* some other boy,
And not my very self, with whom
  The muses used to toy.

For if one's known to jingle *rhymes*,
   Men vote him but a flat,
And pass him with a distant bow,
   And cold enough at that;
But the melody of jingling *dimes*
   Is quite another sound,
That lifts the beavers from their heads
   In deference profound.

Gain is the Ogre of the age,
   That changes men to churls,
And swallows up aspiring minds,
   As oysters swallow pearls;
They leave the bar, the bench, the desk,
   The academic shade,
And, harnessed in alluring bands,
   Become the slaves of trade.

Behold—with solemn "charges" filled—
   Those folios overhead;
Charges against all sorts of men,
   And some against the dead!
These are the records of my life,
   For weary days and years—
A sort of sea where long have swayed
   My shifting hopes and fears.

Yet is my nature not subdued
  To that in which it works;
Mine is a sort of holy war,
  Like NICHOLAS with the Turks!
Like him I quit a peaceful realm
  And seize the battle brand,
That I may add to my domain
  My neighbor's rood of land.

Rhymes are not rhino here:—but trade
  Adds to one's private *weal*,
And bids e'en beef and puddings smoke
  Upon my bit of deal!
So when these kindly questions come,
  As come they do by dozens,
I answer in this way to all
  Enquiring friends and COZZENS.

A *nom de plume*'s a clever vail
  For writers who are shy,
Wherein the private I can meet
  Nor fear the public eye.
I lift the mask for you to peep,
  But charge you not to tell
Who 'tis that dabbles thus in rhyme
  And signs it HONEYWELL.

Printed in Dunstable, United Kingdom

82202526R00114